DATE DUE

THE PROBLEM OF
Miracle
IN PRIMITIVE
CHRISTIANITY

ANTON FRIDRICHSEN

translated by

Roy A. Harrisville and
John S. Hanson

AUGSBURG PUBLISHING HOUSE
Minneapolis, Minnesota

THE PROBLEM OF MIRACLE IN
PRIMITIVE CHRISTIANITY

Contents

Foreword

I welcome this opportunity to reminisce about my great teacher and master Anton Fridrichsen, and to reflect on his contribution to the study of the New Testament and the history of early Christianity. For he was a truly great teacher and enabler, an exegete with unusual sensitivity, and with an intellectual restlessness that made it impossible for him to produce the encompassing tomes that become the milestones of scholarship and make their authors' names household words in the seminaries. His media were lectures to students and pastors, letters to colleagues, and the notes and observations—he liked to call them by the humble word "miscellanies"—that he made his favorite format in the numerable publications he started and sponsored. The book here published in English translation and his thesis on Hagios—Qados were his only "books."

It could be argued that to Fridrichsen the synthetic visions—of which he had powerful ones—

were too tentative to be printed. They belonged to the oral medium, the lecture. When he tried to put them on paper, his subtle mind found too many shortcomings. The sin of sins to him was reductionism, and any attempt at a comprehensive vision reduced the reality that fascinated him in its full complexity.

And so he became a man who *wrote* mainly about philological details—not because he was a pedant, only because he saw and felt the immensity of the big questions. In this respect he was very similar to Arthur Darby Nock (who also wrote only two "books"), and it is not surprising that they were in constant correspondence, exchanging "miscellanies." And as Nock fed much of his scholarship into the footnotes of Martin Nilsson's *Geschichte der Griechischen Religion,* so Fridrichsen was doing the same to Walter Bauer's lexicon to the New Testament. Bauer was another of those scholars with whom Fridrichsen was in frequent correspondence.

To the students at Uppsala during the 30s and 40s Fridrichsen was *the* stimulation. For me it is not sacrilegious to use the words of the Emmaus disciples when I try to catch the glow of those days: Did not our hearts burn within us while he talked to us on the road, while he opened to us the scriptures! It was his charisma that made so many of us return to doctoral work in New Testament. Theologically we have been a varied lot over the years. Many of us ended up abroad: Olof Linton in Copenhagen, Gösta Lindeskog in Åbo/Turku, Bo Reicke in Basel, Edvin Larsson in Oslo, Bertil Gärtner at Princeton, and I came to Harvard. Nils

Dahl at Yale was much influenced by him, not least during his stay in Uppsala during the war years. And Harald Riesenfeld inherited Fridrichsen's chair at Uppsala. There were many more (see the series *Acta Seminarii Neotestamentici Upsaliensis*). In addition, Fridrichsen was a major force in continuing education for the clergy—long before there was a term for it he established seminars in the various dioceses and helped many ministers to complete their doctorates while in the parish.

As I re-read his 1925 study on miracles, I am intrigued by the similarities and differences between Fridrichsen and Bultmann. Both had a very similar academic schooling (in Germany, where Fridrichsen went from his native Norway); both were deeply versed in the history of Hellenistic religion and culture—they belonged to the generation that had not been lured by "biblical theology" into believing that a smattering of Hebrew and Judaica allowed the New Testament scholar to dispense with the classics. Both were under the impact of form criticism à la Norden as well as à la Gunkel. Both were unafraid of raising and feeling within themselves the radical questions of historical criticism. In addition, they were in correspondence over the years.

The casual observer may get the impression that Bultmann with his demythologizing is the more radical of the two while Fridrichsen—especially in his later years—was the more conservative. But I doubt that such adjectives and labels help us much here. The point at issue lies differently, I think. The two agreed as to the nature of the Gospels and consequently about the impossibility of historical knowledge of Jesus' personality, etc. But it seems to me that this fact "bothered" Fridrichsen less than it does Bultmann. Hence Fridrichsen did not feel the urge toward distilling a timeless and ultimate and kerygmatic message, purified from myth and "primitive" religious sentiments. He was willing to accept the uncertainty, and he was not troubled by, but found fascinating and beautiful the "nimbus" that surrounded those who had been "the companions and intimate friends of the Son of God" (below, p. 38).

To Fridrichsen this was not a clever way to avoid the hard questions of what actually had happened and can happen. It was a conscious attempt at doing justice to religious experience. In this sense Fridrichsen was less of a theologian and more a historian or phenomenologist of religion. Behind that difference in Fridrichsen lay the theological conviction that genuine faith and vital religion is and will remain mythical, miraculous, and resistant to theological reductionism—orthodox, conservative, liberal, or radical.

I think that most of what Fridrichsen wrote and said was grounded in this respect for and fascination with *homo religiosus*—not least the "little man," the average men and women of faith. (Also in this respect he had much in common with Arthur Darby Nock who had little patience with theologians who thought they could make religion respectable). In speaking about the evangelists in this book, Fridrichsen often refers to them as having "tact," a not very common word in descriptions of this kind. But tact, tenderness, awe, and the like are the marks of Fridrichsen's studies.

Such a style of theological work and biblical interpretation could be criticized as a piece of romanticism. Personally, I would not mind that accusation if that is the price an academic theologian has to pay for remaining in touch with genuine religious experience, and for resisting the reductionisms by which he can feel better in command of his material. To be sure, we need criteria by which to sort out what helps church and society toward religious health *and* vitality. Reductionism achieves health by making theology antiseptic—and sterile. That is safe, but it is not life. . . .

KRISTER STENDAHL

Harvard Divinity School
Cambridge, Massachusetts

Introduction

In recent years, the great majority of New Testament scholars have given their attention to the individuality and theological creativity of the Gospel writers. With such study, the primary concern is to restore to the biblical writer his true identity as an "author-personality." The writer—his peculiarities, his concerns, his theology has now appeared front and center.

But with all this concentration upon what has been called "redaction criticism," the significant work of an older, earlier generation—some of it still pursued by a gifted few—is on the point of being forgotten. In that earlier time, the battle-cry was "form criticism"—a sociological-historical study of the various units of the biblical tradition; their classification as to shape and type or species, and the attempt to fix their origin in a situation of the Christian community in which they circulated in non-literary, oral fashion. At such a stage, when Christian traditions were handed down piecemeal, from mouth to mouth, long before assuming written form, miracle-stories, conflict-speeches, parables and the like were not the expression of a single author-personality, but of the faith and life-expression, the "conversation" of an anonymous community, the faith and life of "Israel" or of the "primitive Christian community."

It was 19th century research that furnished the thrust or stimulus for this concentration on the oral period lying back of the biblical documents. That century was a time when the most profound and widespread transformation of life occurred by use of the power-driven machine and its anonymous manufacture. "Form Criticism" is a child of the industrial revolution, an era marked by attention to end-products and their assembly by anonymous communities of laborers. Let the steam locomotive furnish an example. One unnamed and unsung group bothered its head with converting heat into energy by the manufacture of torques; another with the production of boilers for housing steam; another with the casting of wheels; another with the fitting of torques to crankshafts; still another with the fitting of wheels to axles, *et voilà!*—the locomotive, the *Gemeindebildung*, the community—an anonymous community—formulation!

In such a time, it was almost certain that men would turn their attention from the creation of individual genius to the item manufactured by the nameless mass; almost certain that in one way or another that mass should itself become the object of investigation. "Workingmen"—not Matthew, Mark or Luke—"workingmen of all countries,

unite!" The concentration lay on the *Gemeinde*, the
community and its *Bildung*, its product—the community and its formulation or manufacture was the
thing in ordinary life. And why should it not be so
in the area of the theological? At any rate, the period in question saw a welter of investigation into
the deposits of material husbanded by earliest,
anonymous Christianity—into 1 Peter, say, as reflecting early baptismal practice; into the deposit of
catechetical material and hymnic material produced
by early Christianity, into the deposit of creeds and
credal confessions in the Testaments.

The method of form-critical study was the comparative method, and therein lay its strength and
its weakness. The form critic was trained in the
History of Religions School which spurned any connection with the Enlightenment or Romanticism,
declared its independence from liberalism, and in
good and evil days insisted on Old and New Testament religion as a piece of history. In his attempt
to get back of the written Gospels to their oral antecedents and to fix the "laws of folk psychology"
operative in the development of the oral tradition
prior to its attaining written form, he had little
option but to compare the histories of analogous
traditions in other religions and to conclude that
Gospel tradition must not merely have developed in
like fashion but may actually have been dependent
upon those alien, religious impulses for its own
evolution.

Indeed, if the faith of primitive Christianity was
of a piece with history, then it did not exist in a
vacuum, but was subject to the influences and pres-

sures, mediate or immediate, of friend and foe. Naturally, it was conceded that the similarity between e.g., the miracle narratives in the Gospels and Jewish or Hellenistic wonder-tales, between Jesus' miracles and the stories of miracle-working rabbis or of Apollonius of Tyana did not require drawing the conclusion that one was dependent upon the other in a literary way. Nevertheless, almost exclusive use of the comparative method suggested such a notion. For this reason, scholars of a conservative cast viewed and still view form critical study with great suspicion. Some still use the method only to classify the various units of anonymous tradition, but delay or downright refuse judgment as to the genuineness or inauthenticity of a particular unit (a comparison of K. L. Schmidt's *Der Rahmen der Geschichte Jesu,* 1919, and Martin Dibelius' *Formgeschichte,* 4th ed. 1961, with Bultmann's *The History of the Synoptic Tradition* indicates greater caution on the part of the former in the manner of evaluating the historicity of the units of tradition).

Beneath this penchant for drawing conclusions concerning literary or ideational relationships between one developing religious tradition and another lay a commitment of a philosophical sort. It was the idea that two similar or all but identical events, persons, or things could not occur or exist without the one being directly or indirectly influenced by the other. If Orville and Wilbur Wright flew from Kitty Hawk and Louis Bleriot kept his flying machine aloft near Paris at roughly the same period of history, it was either because they had compared notes or had shared the same *Zeitgeist* which had determined that year X was the year for flying. This view has sometimes been associated with monism, according to which the world of reality is conceived as uniform, indivisible and wholistic— all events are either a single pebble thrown into the water and from which all the ripples in the pond derive, or are merely of those ripples caused by the single stone. From such a view of reality, the spontaneous, irrational, and contingent is absent. It is no secret that in light of the results of its all but exclusive use of the comparative method, the school of comparative religions was hard put to describe the uniqueness of Jesus Christ and of Christian faith. That uniqueness it finally located in Jesus' "personality," his "faith" or "filial relation to God." In his now celebrated essay of 1941 ("The New Testament and Mythology") Bultmann exposed the concentration of this school upon Jesus' religion or religious consciousness as a throwing out of the baby with the wash, and despite his radical criticism asserted that the Gospel tradition was unique in genre. Yet the commitment to a wholistic view, according to which no two events can occur without the one harking back to the other, however mediately, remained unchallenged.

On the other side of the ledger, the enrichment resulting from this type research cannot be overestimated. While it may have induced some to advocate a wholism and others to embrace a type Christianity which had anciently boasted of its existence prior to the Bible and thus its capacity to live without it, this painstaking study of forms and types gave others historical reinforcement to their acknowledgement that neither Bible nor church may live without the other; that while the church, whether of Israel or of Christ, gave birth to the written documents of Scripture, that oral Word, proclaimed and confessed and now congealed in written, literary form, gave birth to the church. That emphasis upon the theology of the Word so characteristic of the dialectical theologian early in this century, and the restoration of exegesis and biblical interpretation to their rightful place within the theological disciplines, was nothing but the twin to form criticism.

To this portrait of form criticism and the form critic, the author of this volume bears striking similarities and differences. As were his German counterparts, Anton Fridrichsen was educated in an intellectual climate hospitable to critical research. His teacher was Lyder Brun of the faculty at the University of Oslo, then Christiania, the "liberalism" of which ultimately induced the conservative element of that institution to break off and form its own theological school. Following his undergraduate training at Oslo, Fridrichsen studied with Ernst von Dobschütz at Breslau, scene of the activity of Rudolf Otto and William Wrede—two of the greatest *Religionsgeschichtler* of them all—and later (1916) of the young docent Rudolf Bultmann who penned his *History of the Synoptic Tradition* there. In the same year, Fridrichsen heard Paul Wendland at Göttingen, birthplace of the History of Religions School, first manned by those giants Wilhelm Bousset, Hermann Gunkel, Johannes Weiss,

Paul Wernle, Wrede and later Wilhelm Heitmüller—
the second, third, and last Bultmann's teachers, and
the first his predecessor at Giessen. Indeed, the
paths of Fridrichsen and Bultmann were sufficiently
parallel and their personal relationships warm
enough for the latter to dedicate the second volume
of his collected essays to "Anton Fridrichsen, faithful friend in good and evil days" *(Glauben und
Verstehen, Gesammelte Aufsätze,* Zweiter Band,
1952). *Le Problème du Miracle,* a dissertation pre-
pared for the theological faculty at Strasbourg, a
school which consciously cultivated connections with
Anglo-Saxon, Scandinavian and Swiss theology, follows as logically from Fridrichsen's intellectual
training as night from day. Judging from the in-
numerable references to it since its publication in
1925, this pioneering piece on the synoptic miracles
was Fridrichsen's most significant work. In light of
its use, it is singular and strange that *Le Problème*
never saw a second edition or a translation into
German and English.

Fridrichsen did not undertake this study of miracle merely because the topic still remains the moot-
est point of all in New Testament study. He was
convinced that miracle was part and parcel of the
oldest Christian faith and mission, that a position
or stance regarding the miraculous was thus required of earliest Christianity. The reason for this
Fridrichsen located in the church's conviction that
it was living in the end-time, that the final cataclysm
and new creation were already being anticipated in
the deeds of Jesus and his followers. For the sake
of this primitive, eschatological hope, Fridrichsen

roundly states that any description of the church's early existence apart from attention to miracle is impossible. Here, certainly, the reader will note a theme of current preoccupation, and struck far in advance of it. Because he maintained this strict correlation of miracle and the eschatological, Fridrichsen insisted upon the messianic character of Jesus' activity, contending that the tradition of the Gospels regarding Jesus' self-consciousness had passed intact through the fires of criticism (Fridrichsen asserted, however, that Jesus did not *publicly* proclaim himself Messiah, so as to break from the traditionally Jewish, messianic scheme; cf. *This is the Church,* ed. Anders Nygren, transl. Carl C. Rasmussen, 1952, p. 26). This viewpoint distanced him from many of his contemporaries, but has come to new expression in our own time.

The goal of this little volume, anticipated in a brief postscript to an essay by S. Eitrem on the temptation of Jesus ("Die Versuchung Christi," *Norsk Teologisk Tidsskrift,* 24 Aargang, 1923-1924), is simply to determine what problems emerged so as to produce a critical attitude toward miracle in the great church, i.e. to answer the question why the source of miracles eventually ran dry. To approach his goal, Fridrichsen saw the necessity of orienting himself to the study of Christian tradition viewed as devout witness, as the expression of the church's faith and religious experience. In other words, he was concerned with what Joachim Jeremias of Göttingen has called the "second situation-in-life" or *Sitz-im-Leben* of the Christian community. Like every other form critic, he believed he could penetrate back of the written Gospels to their oral antecedents, to that period in which evangelic tradition took shape under the influence of the cultic and religious demands of the community, and in accordance with what he called the "epical laws governing popular tradition." What he saw there was a richer and far more varied tradition than the source analysts of his time—working almost exclusively with the written documents—would allow. To Fridrichsen's mind, that early, oral period embraced at least two moods, the one a popular, naive view of the miraculous which eventually was unable to withstand the more subtle attacks of the church's enemies and imitators, and the other a "religious tact" which subjected the earlier tradition to a stylized redaction and in doing so curbed and, a century later, suppressed it.

Unlike friends and counterparts, Fridrichsen was not so sanguine as to believe his form-critical tool could yield an answer to the question of historicity in every instance. He was of the opinion that the *questio facti* ought to be held in abeyance. Thus, the reader of this volume will often encounter a word of caution against attempting to define what is possible in the area of the historical. Putting the matter in Christological terms, Fridrichsen wrote that "we will never succeed in clearly separating the image of Christ from the concrete traits of Jesus' essential character," though he added that beneath the church's witness the "character of Jesus" shines with a brilliant radiance. Fridrichsen denied scholarship to this "character," however, contending the student could only stand in awe of it—the personality of Jesus exceeded the limits of scientific investigation (later Fridrichsen refused such an attempt from a theological standpoint, asserting that whoever followed the "back to Jesus!" slogan would go past Jesus and land in the synagogue; cf. *The Root of the Vine, Essays in Biblical Theology,* 1953, p. 40). On the other hand, though no less critical, Fridrichsen was of a far less sceptical turn of mind than members of the old liberal school or, for that matter, than his friend Bultmann, for whom the skeptical temper of the History of Religions School appeared to have become a methodology. Now and again, Fridrichsen will describe a narrative as fixed in a historical occasion (cf. his remarks on Jesus' injunction to silence in Mark 1:43ff.; on the disciples' surprise at the demons' subjection to them, and on Paul's hymn in 1 Corinthians 13), and contend that the entire eschatological mood of the Christian community with which the miraculous stands or falls is the line of which Jesus himself forms the point of departure. In the last analysis, however, it was that early redaction of the popular faith, a redaction or revision ultimately reflected in the written documents, which claimed Fridrichsen's attention, and rendered the question as to what really happened secondary. There, our author takes his place alongside the other great form critics of western Europe.

Fridrichsen's study led him to differ not only with friends and contemporaries, but with his own earlier opinions. If Jesus himself was aware of the messianic character of his deeds, and if the esoteric nature of his teaching was the result of his countrymen's insensitivity to spiritual things and not at all a theologoumenon superimposed upon the ancient tradition, then William Wrede's interpretation of the "messianic secret" was patently false. And, if 1 Corinthians 13 actually reflected Paul's unease at the spiritual eccentricities and exaggerations of the church at Corinth, then Fridrichsen's own earlier view of that chapter as an interpolation was false as well. This candor in Fridrichsen in the matter of admission of error not only distinguishes him in temperament, but gives the clue to his ability to "sit loose" to the pressures of contemporary trends.

In the last analysis, what guaranteed Fridrichsen's essential independence is that which renders him contemporary and *Le Problème* worth reading. He was one of the earliest to contend that without according a fundamental eschatological conception to the early Christian community, all interpretation of the New Testament goes awry. In 1916, Fridrichsen undertook a philological investigation of the concept of holiness *(Hagios-Qados, Ein Beitrag zu den Voruntersuchungen zur Christlichen Begriffsgeschichte)*. One of the fundamental aspects of that idea Fridrichsen termed its "eschatological coloration," a coloration he suggested had adhered to the idea from the very beginning and which furnished the soil for Israel's ethical consciousness, with the result that holiness as the exponent of Israel's reaction to the world around it was appropriated by the Christian community, though now freed from local and historical tradition. For Fridrichsen this same relation of eschatological to ethical characterized the Hellenistic wing of the Jerusalem Christian community, the wing to which Paul came to be attached and for the sake of which he endured such bitter antagonism from Judaistic agitators ("Die Apologie des Paulus Gal. I," *Paulus und die Urgemeinde*, Zwei Abhandlungen von Lyder Brun und Anton Fridrichsen, 1921). In his brief essay, "The Apostle And His Message" (1947), Fridrichsen wrote that without taking into consideration the fundamental eschatological conception according to which Paul enjoyed a peculiar position reserved for him, neither the apostle's self-consciousness nor his arguments and actions could be understood. In *The Root of the Vine*, Fridrichsen lauded Albert Schweitzer as the first to discern the tremendous consequences of eschatological interpretation for biblical scholarship, and placed him alongside Ferdinand Christian Baur as a pioneer in research. He asserted that the theology of the turn of the century, with its evolutionist view of history, its psychological method of interpretation and its personal idealism had to be rejected in favor of a "surrender" to the eschatological understanding. But it was precisely such an interpretation that led Fridrichsen to repudiate Schweitzer's view of Paul's doctrine of justification as an auxiliary of his thought, and to contend that the apostle's teaching lay at the heart of the message and life of Jesus for whom the ultimate question was that of faith in and obedience to the eschatological message. What was left for Paul, then, was to interpret the meaning of the situation created by the Messiah's coming, i.e. to view the significance of the eschatological condition after the resurrection from the aspect of righteousness.

Fridrichsen's concept of the church which, according to the brief biography in *Religion in Geschichte und Gegenwart* (3rd Edition, Volume 2, 1132f.) formed the center of his "realistic" interpretation of the Bible, was not primarily a sociological or ecclesiological, but rather an eschatological concern. His insistence that Jesus intended to establish the church sprang from his prior conviction that Jesus' activity was not exhausted in the prophetic—the proclamation of the kingdom—but embraced the messianic as well: the creation of the *ecclesia* of the Son of man, "living on the frontier between this world and the world that is to come, sharing with the crucified and risen Son of man a fellowship which encompasses both life and death" *(This is the Church,* p. 35). Thus the church as Jesus Christ in oneness with his people on earth was intelligible only from an eschatological point of view. This in turn provided the presupposition for the apostolic ministry (cf. *ibid.,* pp. 40ff.).

Ultimately, this attention to the eschatological in Fridrichsen's interpretation of Jesus' life and message as well as of the remainder of the New Testament enabled him to stand free of the intra-party strife among members of the History of Religions School who were determined to find Jesus rooted in Jewish theology or interpreted the New Testament in terms of the influence of Hellenistic or other alien religion.

Such a volume as this, markedly anticipatory of current, contemporary discussion; reflecting a scholarship clearly cognizant of its limits; self-critical and unhampered by alien or hidden commitment to a single school, though highly appreciative of any; free of dogmatic embarrassment at using the contributions of men with whom the author fundamentally disagreed, marks it as unique and justifies its perennial use.

The reader will note that in keeping with the original, footnotes occasionally appear in the body of the text, not merely at the end of the volume, and that for ready reference, patristic quotations in Latin and Greek appear in translation from *The Ante-Nicene Fathers,* an old but still useful aid.

In conclusion, the translators express their thanks to Dr. Marianna Forde of St. Paul, Minn., for reviewing the manuscript and making important corrections.

ROY A. HARRISVILLE

Preface

The miracles, or Jesus' acts of supernatural power, occupy a large place in the Gospel narratives and form one of the essential features of the oldest portrait of Christ. For this reason, historical criticism of the New Testament must study these narratives thoroughly and attempt to grasp their fundamental character.

For two centuries the question of Jesus' miracles has divided theological schools. By the use of various methods, criticism of the liberal school has sought to reduce the significance of the miracle stories. It has tried to give them a "natural" explanation or has assigned them a mythological and allegorical origin, or again, has viewed them as having arisen spontaneously from popular faith and imagination. The orthodox school defends Jesus' miracles as proofs of his divinity. It interprets the miracles as part of the larger problem of the relation between the "natural" and "supernatural," the result being a philosophical apologetic of miracle. The orthodox school is not content with liberalism's conceding historicity to a certain group of narratives, i.e. those of healing, which can be explained by the influence of the moral over the physical. The liberal interpretation, of course, reckons with an extraordinary and elusive factor, but, the orthodox tell us, for Jesus as for God, we must allow for absolute power; only this type view corresponds to the ideas of primitive Christianity and to Christian faith in general.

Must we follow liberals and conservatives in putting the question as they do? In other words, must we accept the notion of reality peculiar to a certain modern tendency or must we adhere to an apologetic based on this same notion of reality? If there were not another alternative, the study of the tradition which regards Jesus as thaumaturge would only be of moderate interest and it would be tedious to add anything to the already vast literature on the subject.[1]

It is possible, however, to remain free of these schools. It was liberal theology's great service to have emancipated New Testament science from a naive conception of tradition and to have furnished it with the comparative method in the history of religions. But its criticism takes special interest in *facts* as such. What actually happened, and how did these things take place? Insufficient account has been taken of the religious life and experiences which these narratives record. When it was stated that these narratives were "inauthentic" or legendary, once given this stamp, there was nothing left to say. But what was essential was thereby brushed aside. For what matters above all is a thorough understanding of the religion of primitive Christianity.

But what becomes of the *questio facti?* In the last analysis, is not our goal to establish what is historical in the tradition of Jesus?

It is necessary for us to ask how far we may proceed in such a direction. First of all, is it possible, given this order of things, to gain even approximate historical certitude on any single point? Then, even if we can prove that a considerable portion of the texts go back to the narratives of eyewitnesses who wished to relate exactly what they believed they had seen, who will be able to say what really took place? The question ought thus to be held in abeyance. For establishing a dogmatics of miracles, a solid historical basis is totally lacking. On the other hand, we are unable to recommend a method which can accurately circumscribe the realm of the possible. Our confidence in the scientific understanding of reality is not as naive today as it was formerly. We have become quite skeptical even with respect to the scientific understanding of nature. The result is that we are not less critical of the historical narratives, but less skeptical than the liberal school.

Seen from this perspective, the *questio facti* loses much of its importance. Jesus undoubtedly healed those who were sick and those commonly called demoniacs. Those around him belived they were witnesses to his wonders. But the difficulties begin when we ask "what happened" and "how did these things happen?" At bottom, this is a mystery. What we can ascertain is the impression produced by the

"miracles" and the stylized redaction to which the
tradition subjected them. This is all we can discover
in historical study. Except for a few narratives of
a concrete and indisputably historical character, and
others of a manifestly legendary or plainly tenden-
tious character, the extent and manner in which
religious tradition reflects genuine facts in each of
its features can be seen only vaguely through the
shadows of the past.

Historical and documentary criticism of the Gospels will then resolutely orient itself to the study of
the tradition viewed as devout witness, as an expression of faith and religious experience. The intimate connection between the religious life of primitive Christianity and the historical Jesus ought not
be denied. But we are unable to grasp it. We will
never succeed in clearly separating the image of
Christ from the concrete traits of Jesus' essential
character, nor in tracing the line of development
from one to the other. Scientific investigation can
only examine the religious ideas and motifs of the
tradition. Thus the first requirement is a precise
understanding of the milieu in which this tradition
developed, and secondly, the study of forces which
created the fixed and definitive form of the tradition.

Only after these data are considered does scientific investigation perceive the personality they reveal, or the activities at their base. It does so with
greater or lesser clarity and according to whether
a *speech* or a *narrative* is involved. It is much easier
to raise the question of authenticity where only a
transmitted speech is concerned. For then we are
considering not only the exterior but also the "inner

form," to use the terminology of K. Reinhardt
(Poseidonios, Munich, 1921; cf. the remarks of H.
Leisegang, *Der Apostel Paulus als Denker,* Leipzig,
1923, p. 4, n. 2). Each speech transmitted to us will
be considered authentic insofar as it accords with
the mental structure manifest in the tradition as a
whole, and is in some way the "projection from out
of the center of a most profound reality and its sym-
bolical expression."

But however fertile the principle formulated by
Reinhardt might be, as a *critical* principle it is not
without its drawbacks. His book on Poseidonios
gives proof of this. Carried away by an idolizing of
the "inner form," the author has confined the spiritual reality to very narrow limits and has altogether
diminished the scope of the possible in the area of
the historical. Here science enjoins us to great caution. We must continually consider the possibility
of the formation of a vast secondary tradition, and
also the fact that a union of contradictory ideas,
tradition and original, can be found in the same historical personality.

On the basis of the utterances transmitted, it is
impossible to reconstruct Jesus' entire religious personality with any certainty. Criticism is obliged to
desist in the face of too many questions which will
remain problematic and insoluble. But through the
inner form there shines with brilliant radiance the
character of Jesus, that changeless jewel which no
criticism can impair. And beneath the varied and
multiform traits of devout tradition, particularly
in the miracle stories, we sense the depths of divinity, a prodigious and mystical reality. We have

neither the right nor the ability to deal with it. But we can and should stand in awe of it, all the while analyzing the tradition itself—a feeble reflection of a sublime reality, refracted through opaque prisms —trying to comprehend the experience of the first Christians and the expression they gave it. If, on the other hand, science wishes before all else to study Jesus' personality in light of our psychology, to understand it by means of modern categories of reality, it exceeds its limits and does violence to religion, and, in the end, clears the way for a radical agnosticism or a vague mysticism, or both at the same time.

If we then begin the study of the New Testament miracle narratives apart from all dogmatic bias, a rich and interesting field opens up for investigation. Here we touch one of the more sensitive nerves of the ancient church's piety. From the viewpoint of tradition, the miracle narratives are an extremely fertile and varied area. We cannot set them in one and the same category, since they include very different elements both as to content and form. From the literary standpoint, they are classified among what are usually termed the "apophthegms" (speeches set within a certain frame) and narratives proper. They have been referred to as "paradigms" or "novellas" according to whether the edifying or legendary element predominates (cf. the important book of M. Dibelius, *From Tradition to Gospel,* New York, 1965, and K. L. Schmidt in *Festschrift für Hermann Gunkel,* Göttingen, 1923, p. 131). It would be necessary to see how each narrative is formed and to seek to establish a classification according to the principles of form criticism. This study would have to be linked to an analysis of fragments taken from the history of religions, assembling as many of the comparative materials as possible. Finally, all these observations and reflections might conclude with a medical and psychological evaluation.[2]

The study about to be undertaken has no intention of exhausting the subject. The goal proposed is limited. We will confine ourselves to indicating and explaining *general ideas* about the miracles to the degree they were presented to the church of the faithful as one of the aspects of the character and activity of Jesus Christ. Our procedure will thus differ from that which examines each narrative separately. We begin with the entirety of Jesus' personality as given us in the Gospels, and ask what place the miracles occupy there. But we must not expect to find a definitive answer, one which would express in a single and simple formula primitive Christianity's notion of miracle. This part of Jesus' activity has not been judged equally in all places and at all times.

Alongside naive delight in miracle, sources of the synoptic tradition already furnish us an appreciation and more reflective use of the *dynameis*. The acts of power form the point of departure and the background for the important *speeches* of Jesus. In the course of the Christian mission, pious reflection necessarily developed further, giving rise to a messianic dogmatics and apologetic, and to which the historical tradition had to be accommodated. In what light are Jesus' miracles cast, when are they considered acts of the Son of God, the Messiah, the Savior? We will first seek an answer to this question.

In examining the sources for this purpose, we observe one interesting and important factor: Jesus' miracles have occasionally given Christian apology considerable *difficulties*. The *dynameis* were interpreted in hostile and malevolent fashion by the opponents of Christian faith, who hurled at Jesus the thaumaturge slanders which were extremely embarrassing to the faithful and to the Christian mission. What traces remain in the oldest tradition due to the dispute evoked by these calumnies? We will bring this to light in the second section of our study.

The problem of miracle in primitive Christianity was not only apologetic in nature but also concerned the church's religious life properly so-called. That period knew of no rationalism which would put the reality of miracle in doubt. All were imbued with the ardent conviction that the *dynameis* of Christ were operative in the believers. But from its earliest beginnings, the Christian religion also included non-miraculous elements—penitence and the remission of sins, the new commandment and suffering. If enthusiasm, the cult of miracle tended naturally to a certain hypertrophy, such an exclusive development, so dangerous to the religious and moral life, had to be counter-balanced by defining the limits of thaumaturgy and by stressing the predominant importance of faith and life. In studying miracle in the early church, we must also examine the problem under this aspect.

Our study is divided into three sections:

I. The evaluation of Jesus' miracles in primitive Christianity.

II. Criticism hostile to Jesus' miracles.

III. The problem of miracle in the church.

I.

The Evaluation of Jesus' Miracles in Primitive Christianity

It is a rather curious but indisputable fact that Jesus' miracles are very rarely mentioned outside the four Gospels. We are obliged to recognize and to seek an explanation for this, and from this viewpoint must investigate the synoptic Gospels as to their literary and historical character. But before considering the principal problem, that of knowing what the first Christians thought of Jesus' miracles, we ought to pose another question: What role did miracle play in the primitive Christian mission? Then we shall approach the problem of interest to us here and attempt to assign Jesus' miracles their place within the whole of the messianic portrait presented by the Gospel tradition. We will conclude by examining Jesus' own utterances concerning his *dynameis.*

PRIMITIVE CHRISTIAN INTEREST IN THE LIFE OF JESUS

The interest which history inspires in us today was unknown to primitive Christianity. Our thought

33

is dominated by the principles and methods of modern science whose purpose is to study facts and uncover relationships. We view the past with a gaze which criticism has rendered keen and penetrating so as to grasp the origin, formation, and development of phenomena. The first Christians lived in the present. What interested them was the actual, transcendent reality: ΚΥΡΙΟΣ ΙΗΣΟΥΣ. The celestial Christ at the right hand of the Father was the object of their faith and hope. They found him in common worship; he lived in them, and they proclaimed him in their missionary preaching.

It is true that history occupied a certain place in the religious thought of primitive Christianity, but in a particular way. What is history for us, the life of Jesus and his activity, was for the first Christains only one act and that not even the principal act in the great drama of salvation. Their interest centered chiefly in the facts of the incarnation, death, resurrection and glorification of Christ. Set among these awesome events which shared in the transcendent world, Jesus' earthly activity and the details of his life appeared to be little more than subordinate facts.

Yet we would be grossly mistaken if we wished to deny primitive Christianity a sense for details of this sort. Each aspect of Jesus' life known or transmitted by the tradition was a precious possession which had been accepted and painstakingly preserved. But the need was not felt to collect these features in order to compose a total portrait of Jesus from them. He was already known, the Lord, the heavenly Son of God, the dead and resurrected one whom men adored. Under these circumstances, the words and acts of Jesus related by the tradition had value principally as illustrations and proofs in the context of worship, preaching and exhortation, that is, as episodes and isolated speeches, and not as fragments of a historical sequence.

This understanding, as we shall explain directly, is proper to all primitive Christianity, to Jewish-Christians and Gentile converts as well. The necessity for drawing a certain distinction between the interests of these two groups regarding the tradition of the life of Jesus is obvious. The Jewish-Christians were the recognized guardians of the tradition of Jesus. As Jews, they lived altogether in sacred history, and in this Jewish world Jesus lived. We note also the development in post-exilic Judaism of interest and taste for the words and deeds of the great teachers, for the Haggada and for rabbinic narratives. But Jewish-Christians and converted heathen have basically the same attitude to the Christian tradition: the narratives of Jesus' life serve the cultus and its ends. The essential data of the religious conscience are the great deeds of redemption unfolding between heaven and earth. Let us describe these circumstances with the help of our sources.

In *Paul* we already encounter these characteristic features. It is useless to explain in detail how all the apostle's attention is centered about the great events of redemption—the incarnation, death and resurrection of Christ. All of Jesus' life between the incarnation and death is summed up in the idea of *humiliation* (Phil. 2:6ff.)—he assumed the form of a servant, humbled himself and became obedient to death on the cross. The way in which Christ's *example* is used for practical life corresponds to the preceding summary conception: We must follow him in humility, meekness, and in giving ourselves to others (Rom. 15:3; 2 Cor. 10:1; 8:9). In sum, he is the great model of goodness and patience in suffering. "Be imitators of me," writes Paul to his church (1 Cor. 11:1) "as I am of Christ. . . ." But this idea of example and imitation approaches that of mystical communion with Christ, which causes the nature of the master as if to overflow into the soul of the believer. We note a later development characteristic of this disposition in the Deutero-Pauline passage in Ephesians 4:20. Here the readers' former pagan life is described (4:18f.) and then in traditional fashion it is said: "You did not so learn Christ!— assuming that you have heard about him and were taught in him, as the truth is in Jesus. Put off your old nature which belongs to your former manner of life. . . ." At first sight, Jesus appears to be viewed as the incarnation of the new life ideal. But if we examine more closely the expressions "to be taught *in Christ*" and "as the truth is in Jesus," it is immediately clear that a teaching of "Christianity" is involved, that consequently Christ or Jesus is not the Jesus of history but the Lord acting through the doctrine and teaching of the church.

In the apostle's attitude to the words and commands of Jesus we note a similar juxtaposition of the transcendental and historical, with the accent on the former. For him these words and commands are the supreme authority to which absolute obedience

is due (1 Cor. 7:10, 25; 9:14). But *Scripture* is an
authority which he invokes still more often (cf. 1
Cor. 9:8ff., where the law is cited as of first importance). Lastly, there are the *revelations* which are
of decisive importance, because they manifest the
present and living Lord (cf., e.g., Paul's teaching
concerning the fate of the dead, 1 Thess. 4:15ff.).

Under these circumstances we cannot disregard
the fact that taken as a whole, the tradition about
Jesus which played so large a role in Palestinian
and Syrian churches had lost much of its importance
for Paul. Today we will very rarely find a theologian
asserting that the apostle could not have known this
tradition; but we can boldly affirm that it was not a
creative and constitutive element of his piety. Further, the formula in 2 Cor. 5:16 is characteristic of
Paul. It forces us to recognize that if he did not
consciously scorn historical detail, he at least emphatically thrust it aside.

Much has been thought and written on this passage;
the most important contributions were furnished by
Johannes Weiss, *Paulus und Jesus,* Berlin, 1909, pp.
23ff.; R. Reitzenstein, *Die hellenistischen Mysterienreligionen,* 2nd ed., 1920, pp. 226ff.; H. Windisch, *Der
Zweite Korintherbrief,* Göttingen, 1924, pp. 184ff.; H.
Lietzmann, Handbuch III, 1, 2nd ed., 1924, pp. 124ff. It
is perhaps advisable to consider more closely a similar
text. The meaning of the apostle's words seems evident
to me. The tone of the fragment in 5:11f. is polemical;
the words are directed against those who "pride themselves on a man's position and not on his heart (vs. 12)."
As for Paul, he lives only for God's cause and for the
good of the churches (vs. 13), because the love of Christ
controls him (vs. 14). He expresses this love (vs. 15)
in a most original formula by declaring that "he died for
all, that those who live might live no longer for them-

selves but for him who for their sake died and was raised." Finally he concludes from it (vs. 16) that "from now on, therefore (ὥστε), we regard no one from a human point of view; even though we once regarded Christ from a human point of view, we regard him thus no longer." This conclusion extends to vs. 17 (ὥστε), but now is given positive form in a principle which distances us from the polemic. So we have only to keep in mind vs. 16 and the context which precedes it.

It is evident, then, that this *general* clause: "we regard no one from a human point of view," does not prepare for the following statement about the Christ who possesses a *special* character, but is set in bold relief by the conditional clause which follows and which leads us to the final outcome. Thus, by the death of Christ, all are dead, and, insofar as they are still alive, they are transported into a sphere superior to that of nature and man (vs. 15). We must conclude that in these new conditions of life (ἀπὸ τοῦ νῦν) "we (ἡμεῖς=all Christians) regard no one from a human point of view." The polemical thrust of these words can only be directed against those who "pride themselves on a man's position," that is, against those who boast of personal acquaintance with the great authorities of Jerusalem, called pillars. They had all sorts of things to relate concerning the apostles —character traits, anecdotes concerning their manner of healing, teaching, replying, praying, executing justice, eating, drinking, sleeping, etc. We usually have but a feeble notion of the immense authority the personal disciples of Jesus (as well as the Lord's relatives) enjoyed in the primitive church. When we read the anecdotes of the rabbis, and see to what extent these narratives were inspired by ardent worship of authorities, we can get an idea of the profound veneration given the apostles of Jesus at the very outset. But in the Hellenistic churches as well the image of these men was surrounded with a nimbus, for they had been the companions and intimate friends of the Son of God. With a truly religious curiosity they gathered every story of the life of the apostles; the smallest detail interested them. We can also observe this mentality in the apocryphal acts of the apostles.

In this regard as in others, Paul isolates himself with a superb independence (see how he reacted to the cult given the person of the apostles in Gal. 2). He shows his independence by refusing to assign any value whatsoever to all these traditions or all these personal and doubtless interesting recollections. What is important to him is the new life, the new creature in Christ. He shapes this thought with extreme resolution by declaring that even personal knowledge of Christ according to the flesh was without real value. The conditional clause εἰ καὶ ἐγνώκαμεν ought then to be construed as referring to a possibility (cf. Gal. 5:11: εἰ περιτομὴν ἔτι κηρύσσω, τὶ ἔτι διώκομαι; and Xenophon, Mem. II, 2, 7: εἰ καὶ πάντα ταῦτα πεποίηκε . . . . οὐδεὶς ἂν δύναιτο αὐτῆς ἀνέχεσθαι τὴν χαλεπότητα): the instance is cited, but without stating it corresponds to any reality.

How was Paul able to reinforce his thought so boldly? It is temperament, clearly, not calm reflection which speaks here, and the chain of ideas came of itself. The cult of the outward person of the apostles spontaneously called attention to him who was above them and could not be surpassed as man—the Lord himself.

But must we see here only the language of temperament? Do not these words actually reveal a certain malaise felt by the apostle in the face of the Gospel tradition and the varied human spectacle it presents? In Matthew and Luke we note how often the all-too-human character of the Markan narratives has been attenuated and tempered (cf. F. Nicolardot, *Les procédés de rédaction des trois premiers évangélistes,* 1908) ; and the Gospel of John presents us with a living image of what should be a compromise between historical recollection and transcendent faith. Paul did not have to inquire into this compromise, which became necessary only later. The apostle could brush aside this difficulty by refusing to regard Christ according to the flesh any longer.

Here is the psychological explanation for the fact that the apostle spoke so little of Jesus' human life, though he knew it quite well. Jesus is not even directly mentioned as *messenger*. Paul makes an allusion here, insofar as εὐαγγέλιον τοῦ Χριστοῦ denotes "the gospel preached by Christ," but here too he is chiefly concerned with the heavenly Lord of mission (cf. O. Schmitz, *Die Christus-Gemeinschaft des Paulus im Lichte seines Genetiv-Gebrauchs*, Gütersloh, 1924, pp. 45ff.). We read in Eph. 2:17 that "he came and preached peace to you who were far off. . . ." But this message was transmitted by the apostles (2 Cor. 5:20: "So we are ambassadors for Christ, God making his appeal through us"). Only once does Paul mention the tradition of the *Last Supper* celebrated by Jesus and his disciples (1 Cor. 11:23ff.), but here Jesus appears as founder of the cult, that is, in a celestial role. When he declares Jesus free from sin (2 Cor. 5:21; Rom. 5:18), it is in the context of a tightly-knit religious dialectic, and not chiefly under the impression of the perfect harmony of Jesus' personality in his action and suffering. It is a great honor for Israel that the Son of God made flesh assumed the outward form of a *Jew* (Rom. 9:5). But this fact too is set in a dogmatic sequence (Gal. 4:4ff.), or it is one of the terms of the "dual kerygma" which, by pitting the one against the other, harmonizes the two forms of

Jesus' existence: born son of David according to the flesh, and Son of God according to the Spirit of holiness (Rom. 1:3ff.).

But what really suits this whole religious point of view is that we frequently encounter the name of Jesus in set formulas of a binary (or ternary) or Christological character. We need merely recall such passages as 1 Thess. 1:1; 1:3; 3:2; 3:11 to show how from this ancient period the ideas of God, Christ and the Holy Spirit are closely and firmly united. The apostle generally begins his letters with wishing his readers "grace and peace from God our Father and the Lord Jesus Christ" (Rom. 1:7; 1 Cor. 1:3; 2 Cor. 1:2). Formulas containing the Christian triad are found, e.g., in 2 Cor. 13:14; 1:21ff. (cf. 1 Cor. 6:11; 12:4ff.). Note also Christological confessions of faith which undoubtedly have a liturgical origin as, e.g., in 1 Cor. 15:3ff.; Phil. 2:5-11; 1 Tim. 3:16; 1 Peter 3:18ff. The transcendental outlook dominates throughout, and the incarnation, death, etc. are subordinated to it.

Paul and the life of Jesus. Of late, this problem has been the source of lively discussion. Among the numerous studies on the question, we refer to W. Wrede, *Paul,* Boston, 1908, pp. 155ff.; Adolf Jülicher, *Paulus und Jesus,* Tübingen, 1907, pp. 30ff. *(Religionsgeschichtliche Volksbücher* I, 14); Albert Schweitzer, *Geschichte der Paulinischen Forschung,* Tübingen, 1911, p. 191; Olaf Moe, *Paulus und die evangelische Geschichte,* Leipzig, 1912; Maurice Jones, *The New Testament in the Twentieth Century,* London, 1914, pp. 36-59; Johannes Weiss, *The History of Primitive Christianity,* (2 vols.), New York, 1937, pp. 452ff.; R. Paulus, *Das Christusproblem der Gegenwart,* Tübingen, 1922, pp. 26ff.; H. Leisegang, *Der Apostel Paulus als Denker,* Leipzig, 1923, pp. 25ff.;

B. W. Bacon, *Is Mark a Roman Gospel?* Cambridge, 1919; *Jesus and Paul,* London, 1921. The problem here is not of analyzing the religious and moral influence of Jesus' personality on the apostle, whether he saw and heard the Lord during his life-time or derived his impressions from the tradition. We are concerned with defining the value he assigned to the human life of Jesus and how he used it in his preaching and teaching.

It is only rarely denied that Paul knew the tradition about Jesus (Wrede, Bacon). It is almost inconceivable that the apostle ignored what was said of the Messiah in Jerusalem, Damascus or Antioch. But how to interpret the fact that he so rarely mentions the historical life of Jesus and never enters into its details? Here, surely, it is not enough to emphasize that his letters were occasioned by circumstances hardly favorable to such allusions. We must thus make clear that with Paul the accent falls on areas of the Christian faith other than the various features of Jesus' life. What is more, with Paul there are motifs which divest such details of all importance. Schweitzer holds that for Paul there is generally no link between the prior epoch of the Lord's death and resurrection and the new era of completed salvation in which everything is of a higher order. Jesus' human life belongs to the old era now abolished and has thus lost its interest. It is then with deliberate purpose that the apostle neglects the life of Jesus (cf. 2 Cor. 5:16). Leisegang arrives at a similar conclusion, but bases it on somewhat different reflections. According to him, Paul sees the same chasm between the man Jesus and the heavenly Christ as between the old and new man, between the ψυχικοί and the πνευματικόι. Thus, the apostle has no interest in the tradition of the human Jesus. "The Christ of Paul is not only wholly other than he who preached the sermon on the mount; he is his complete opposite. That this is so, and cannot be otherwise, is the great *mysterion* revealed to him, and which he must proclaim to men."

I can follow neither the reasoning of Schweitzer nor of Leisegang. What prevents me from doing so, before all else, is the idea which Paul develops of Jesus as the *second Adam*. This idea certainly includes the human life of Jesus (1 Cor. 15; Rom. 5). It is true that Paul opposes the "son of David according to the flesh" to the "Son of God according to the Spirit of holiness," but Leisegang exaggerates the difference by defining it as an absolute contrast; it is rather a relative one. The interpretation Leisegang gives of the passage in Romans 8:3 (God sent his Son ἐν ὁμοιώματι σαρκὸς ἁμαρτίας) cannot be correct. Leisegang thinks the notion is flatly formulated there that Jesus, by becoming man, became also a sinner in the proper sense of the term. But in spite of Romans 5:14, ὁμοίωμα has a certain restrictive sense. And, no doubt, 2 Cor. 5:21 (τὸν μὴ γνόντα ἁμαρτίαν ὑπὲρ ἡμῶν ἁμαρτίαν ἐποίησεν) aims chiefly at Jesus' *death* for men's sins, and not at his sinless life (cf. Windisch in his commentary). Leisegang finds in the ἐκένωσεν ἑαυτόν of Phil. 2:7ff. the counterpart of such formulas as πλήρης θεοῦ, πληρωθῆναι πνεύματος ἁγίου—which is very doubtful. Κενόω, a word often used by Paul, does not have a strictly terminological sense here, and κένωσις refers to the μορφὴ θεοῦ. Even in the σχῆμα δούλου Jesus remains in the state of εἶναι ἴσα θεῷ (cf. A. Fridrichsen, *Revue d'histoire et de philosophie religieuses*, 1923, p. 441f). But we could not say exactly how Paul viewed Jesus' human appearance. On the whole, he characterizes it as a humbling in comparison to the μορφὴ θεοῦ. But did he not find evidence of the Lord's divinity in the features of his human life? This we can establish with a certitude based on clear observations. We will always wonder how Paul found the divinity of the Messiah expressed. In his "humiliation," his *dynameis*, his utterances, or in his εὐεργεσίαι?

However sublime and grandiose the emanations of divinity hidden beneath Jesus' humble form, they were of little satisfaction to the apostle. This is why he goes so far as to say that he does not want to know Christ according to the flesh. This explains perfectly why he rarely cites details from Jesus' life in the discussions and exhortations of his letters.

Nevertheless, we ought not doubt that the acts and words of Jesus had their place, at least to certain extent, in the apostle's missionary preaching and exhortations. This was inevitable in regard to Jews for whom the Messiah obviously had an essential importance.

Paul has detained us a bit longer because he stands at the beginning of the ecclesiastical evolution, and because we see in him the typical traits of a development. Were our observation extended to the second century, we would find no new conception of Jesus' earthly life until we reached the apologists (cf. J. Rouffiac, *La Personne de Jésus chez les Pères apostoliques,* Paris, 1908). The allusions made there are rare. In 2 Peter (1:16ff.), a writing which must be fixed quite late and which mentions the story of the transfiguration, we see this point of view confirmed. This narrative shows us Jesus wrapped in heavenly light. For the rest, there is continual accent on Christ's exemplary attitude in his suffering, meekness, and courage (1 Peter 2:21ff.; 1 Clement, Chap. 16; 1 Tim. 6:13). For *Clement of Rome* (Chap. 42), Jesus' historical role chiefly consists in teaching the apostles and instructing them (concerning the coming kingdom of God), a conception characteristic of ecclesiastical style. Regarding the Lord's earthly activity *The Epistle of Barnabas* (V, 6ff.), expresses itself in these terms:

> And He (since it behoved Him to appear in flesh), that He might abolish death, and reveal the resurrection from the dead, endured (what and as He did), in order that He might fulfill the promise made unto the fathers, and by preparing a new people for Himself, might show, while He dwelt on earth, that He, when He has raised up mankind,

will also judge them. Moreover, teaching Israel,
and doing so great miracles and signs, He preached
(the truth) to him, and greatly loved him. But
when He chose His own apostles who were to preach
His Gospel, (He did so from among those) who
were sinners above all sin, that He might show He
came "not to call the righteous, but sinners to repentance." Then He manifested Himself to be the
Son of God. *(The Ante-Nicene Fathers,* trans. Alexander Roberts and James Donaldson, Buffalo, 1886,
I, 139).

It is obvious that the idea of the public preaching
of Jesus and his miracles is not necessarily linked
to the conception of his redemptive work which was
to destroy death, demonstrate the resurrection and
judgment, fulfill the promises and prepare a new
people. The preaching and the miracles, facts transmitted by the tradition, are as digressions in the
natural sequence of thought and without real relation to the controlling idea.

To the great question, *cur deus homo?* the *Epistle
to the Hebrews* gives the traditional response: He
became man that by his death he might destroy the
devil and deliver men from the fear of death (2:15),
and fulfill his work as high priest. It is clear that
these reflections lead to the idea of the great heavenly priest. But, in addition, a certain contact with
the historical tradition is sensed, not only in regard
to external facts (Jesus was of the tribe of Judah:
7:14; he first preached repentance: 2:3; 6:1ff.; he
aroused a violent opposition on the part of his people: 12:3; he died on the cross: 12:2; 13:12) but
especially in regard to the humiliation of Christ.
The general notion of humility and obedience is

already found in Paul (Phil. 2:8), but our author insists on the meaning of these events for Jesus' person and hence for us (5:7, 8; 2:18; 4:15). This idea, absent in all the literature of primitive Christianity, could have been borrowed from a fixed schematic formula of a pedagogical and parenetic type which construes or explains with primitive naiveté the believer's religious experience as reflecting the inner development of Jesus. Or it is the Hellenistic idea of the σωτήρ which is introduced here: The Redeemer, after having "achieved perfection" by suffering and tribulation, has become fit to aid men in the same sufferings (Hercules, Mithra, etc.).[3]

Next to Holy Scripture (the Old Testament) *the words of Jesus* play an ever-larger role, as we can see from the quotations of the apostolic fathers. This observation is corroborated by the discovery of papyri containing collections of the words of Jesus (the Logia; cf. H.E.J. White, *The Sayings of Jesus,* Cambridge, 1920). But here again the concrete idea gives place to the scheme: Alongside the work of Redeemer (σωτήρ) there is that of lawgiver (νομοθέτης), the other aspect of Jesus' activity. The apostolic fathers and apologists often speak of the law or commandments of Jesus (e.g., Justin, Dialogue 12:2; 14:3; 18:3; Ignatius to the Magnesians, Chap. 2; 2 Clement 3:4; 6:7; cf. Adolf von Harnack, *Mission und Ausbreitung des Christentums* I, 3rd ed., Leipzig, 1915, p. 383, n. 2). This conception goes far beyond the sense of the Pauline expression "the law of Christ" (Gal. 6:2). The Lord is founder of the church (already in Eph. 4:11ff.); he is the author of the Christian moral code. Again we observe how the church fashions history by imposing its own style upon it.

Is there any significance to the fact that the ancient historical conception of Jesus as the master-teacher (διδάσκαλος) has been eclipsed? We do not find the idea in Paul, and rarely elsewhere (Heb. 2:3; 1 Clem. 13:1; Polycarp, ep. 2). "The Lord's teaching to the heathen by the Twelve Apostles" is a document of ecclesiastical law. And when the apologists call Christ master, they are yielding to the terminology of the philosophical schools. No author of this period cites the words of Jesus from the Gospels as often as Justin. For him, Jesus is the head of a school, the founder of the true philosophy, whose δόξαι have the value of a rule of conduct for his disciples (cf. E. R. Goodenough, *The Theology of Justin the Martyr*, Jena, 1923, pp. 250ff.).

In the *apocryphal* literature the strictly religious concern is plainly linked to the penchant for telling anecdotes, exciting attention and diverting the imagination. The details are given loving care. But the historical terrain is abandoned and wild fantasy prevails. This literature continued to be a by-product of the expansion of the church's life, without any superior power to create new forms of life. It was not without influence, however, for it referred to the history, while contributing to the weakening of historical categories and elevating the earthly and human life of Jesus to divine status. We will understand nothing of John's Gospel if we do not take account of this preliminary preparation of popular feeling.

But certainly another factor forced the church to examine the historical tradition more carefully than before, i.e. *Gnosticism.* The devotees of this doctrine declared they had received their teaching and customs from Jesus, communicated and ordained by him in a revelation. They then began to interpret the Gospels, but also created traditions to justify their claims. These formations of Gnostic tradition exerted great influence on the church by arousing interest in the Gospel tradition. No doubt, the zeal with which *Papias* collected the true words of the Lord could not be explained apart from these particular circumstances which in turn led the church to produce works of an analogous form, especially on Coptic soil (e.g., the so-called *Epistula apostolorum,* ed. by C. Schmidt, *Texte und Untersuchungen,* Band 43, Berlin, 1919). In sum, these circumstances stimulated the church to pay greater attention to the old Gospel traditions, for it had to offer criticism of the Gnostic production. The canon of the New Testament and its fourfold Gospel is the result of this critical reflection. The formation of the canon assigned a definite place to the life of Jesus in the church's theology, and from this moment on, cultus, speculation and Holy Scripture are found in steady correlation—dogmatics sides with exegesis. In *Justin, Irenaeus* and *Origen* we see the continual development and modification of the dogma of the primitive church. But we also observe in them all the growing influence of the tradition of the life of Jesus, fixed in writing and canonized. Later, however, it was difficult to introduce this element into the general dogmatic structure. This difficulty is confirmed, to cite but one example, in the struggle between the exegetical schools of Antioch and Alexandria.

THE SYNOPTIC GOSPELS

We have given a brief sketch of the oldest period of the church which lasted approximately a century. We have found that the religious interest of this period showed only feeble interest in the earthly life of Jesus. Knowledge of historical detail had undoubtedly been more or less widespread in the various churches. It is probable that some tradition, at least, existed everywhere. But in the apostolic age this tradition lived as if underground; it dominated neither religious thought nor literature. Under the circumstances, can we form an idea of the points of view applied to the life of Jesus in the Christian mission?

If this is possible, at least to a degree, it is because one part of the church was keenly interested in the various features of the life and activity of Jesus, viz., the churches of Palestine and Syria. These churches yielded the materials to facilitate Gospel composition. And these writings allow us to form a general view of the question examined in this study.

For a study intending to make use of the Gospels as historical sources, it is of greatest importance to have a proper idea of these writings. In approaching such documents, it is a fatal error to put to them questions to which they neither can nor intend to respond. We must concede that criticism long

applied to the tradition a method inappropriate to
the special character of these narratives. At every
turn the question was: Does an eye-witness speak
here, or do we find some sort of tendency in this
narrative or that utterance? The possibility of en-
countering a spontaneous creation of the imagination was often conceded. But we have doubtless
come to a different and fairer understanding of the
synoptic Gospels both as to their contents and their
redaction.

We must definitely dispense with the idea of "re-
membrance" as forming the basis of the Gospels.
Justin, a distinguished Greek, introduced this notion (the ἀπομνημονεύματα of the apostles, Apol. I, 66),
applying to the Gospels a term borrowed from a
literary genre out of harmony with their character
and originating in a totally different culture.[4] The
synoptic narratives are popular in essence. The numerous concrete and flexible details have nothing to
do with that retrospective recollection which faith-
fully reproduces experiences of the past. Rather,
they originate in the art of an artless narrator, who
lacks all literary disposition but is inwardly grasped
by his subject and wishes to grasp others.[5]

Thus, from the point of view we have adopted,
we must modify the notion of "tendency." We must
regard all the narratives and utterances as having
a tendency because they originate in the spiritual
life of the churches (which hardly means that they
produced them). In the last analysis, the stories
and utterances transmitted have but a single tendency, viz., to edify. They intend to instruct, exhort,
stir up, strengthen, support and quicken the one-

ness of mind by giving it concrete expression. With reason, but perhaps with a bit of exaggeration, G. Bertram has spoken of the *cultic* character of this tradition. This means that the tradition took shape chiefly under the influence of the religious needs and circumstances of the church. Even if certain tendencies are present there—and we will indicate some of them in this study—they are not conscious literary tendencies pursuing a certain goal. In almost every instance we must note the expression of some internal problem raised by the contact of piety with the situation of the church.

The conception of the synoptic tradition just outlined has important consequences for our ideas of the *written redaction* of the Gospels. Till very recently, criticism was concerned mainly with *source* analysis. It was thought that the tradition developed in the following manner: Since the earliest period, eyewitness narratives led to the formation of sources; the oral tradition was fixed in small fragments which were later combined into larger wholes. In the course of this history, many elements were inserted which were neither authentic nor original. Criticism then proposed to break down the most important literary components into their integral parts and to eliminate everything secondary. After the "sources" were thus reconstituted by means of minute comparison and all sorts of deliberations, it was believed the historical events as would have occurred could be immediately located.

This source-superstition has been extremely prejudicial to the contemporary study of the Gospels. Immense work has been done in the area of docu-

mentary criticism without obtaining, apart from
some clearly general information, positive results
in the details. Above all, the dogma of the *historical
character of the Gospel of Mark* has been too long
maintained. Even in 1922, a renowned scholar, Ed.
Meyer (in his voluminous work, *Ursprung und
Anfänge des Christentums* I) wished to find in
Mark's Gospel the sources which he thought originated in the circle formed about Peter, sources
which Mark enriched with his own reminiscences
of the apostle. The Gospel, in its essential traits,
should then present a faithful image of the development of Jesus' historical activity.

These illusions must be irrevocably rejected. Between the events and the manuscript of the Gospels,
there is a much more varied and complex tradition.
We must reckon with more than the three phases of
history, sources, and Gospel. What followed the
events themselves was the infinite variety of oral
tradition which transmitted certain facts and utterances whose chief character was fixed by sheer
repetition. But they varied and assumed a certain
shape and style according to the epical laws governing popular tradition. Another phase which we can
distinguish only imperfectly, indicates groupings of
pericopes and utterances which are linked in content as well as in form. Finally, we must consider
the written composition, i.e. the Gospel.

In other words, the development of the Gospel collection is a literary product only in its final phase.
And this final redaction did not at all seek to give
an historical exposé as we understand it. It was
content to gather the scattered and varied materials

into a literary unity. In an important work, K. L. Schmidt has shown that the plan of Jesus' life, as the Gospel of Mark gives it, is only a scheme created by the redactor. The chronological and topographical notes, the frequent brief introductory notes on the pericopes, and the marginal comments by means of which scholars intended to reconstruct the history of Jesus are largely of a literary nature and the work of a redactor who used them to combine the isolated units of the tradition. Mark probably found the passion narrative already in a relatively fixed form; very early cultic needs created a general, uniform structure. The division of other elements of the narrative was given in the nature of the events themselves. The anointing by the Holy Spirit during baptism was the natural point of departure. Further, everything furnished us as chronological, topographical, and other type information may occasionally date back to ancient fragments of oral tradition, but the notes in their entirety are the work of the redactor.

We must judge *Luke's* literary work in similar fashion. He is no more a historian than the others. He is a writer, and compared to Matthew and Mark, of the highest quality. With him the religious interest dominates. He lacks any sense for biography and historical connection. In the prolog to his Gospel (1:1-4), he declares that after having examined all these things from the beginning, it seemed good to him to explain them in writing to Theophilus, "in an orderly account." Actually, Luke has appropriated the style, but not the spirit of Hellenism. The spirit animating him is that of faith. Luke is a de-

vout and believing narrator with a certain taste for
language and style, which by no means alters his attitude vis-a-vis the tradition. He affects a certain
objectivity in speaking of the "things which have
been accomplished among us" (1:1), and intends
that Theophilus acknowledge "the truth concerning
the things of which you have been informed." [6] But
these are only literary phrases, and are not connected with the real content of his two volumes
(cf. Ed. Meyer's opposite observation in his *Ursprung und Anfänge* I, pp. 3ff.; III, pp. 3ff.). What
is peculiar to the third evangelist is above all a
conception which inspires his narrative: He relates
the course of the gospel from the Savior's appearance on earth to the apostle Paul's entry upon the
capital of the world. For Luke, this conception
marks out a vast intellectual horizon and a sense
for the broad outline of history on which the prog-
ress of Christianity was achieved. But in details
Luke does not surpass the naiveté of the synoptic
species. Thanks to his literary taste, he handles
the Greek with a bit more finesse than the others
and composes with greater boldness than Mark and
Matthew. With insufficient and incoherent data, he
knows how to compose a narrative where everything holds together and in sequence (cf. M. Dibelius, *Festschrift Hermann Gunkel,* pp. 27ff.). It is
precisely this sense which is expressed in the prolog when he promises to give the story "in an
orderly account" (καθεξῆς).

The evangelists did not draft their texts with the
historian's method. They did not intend to state
facts, explain relationships, write a biography and

to this end engage in a criticism of the sources. They viewed the tradition from the standpoint of the *universal Christian mission,* in light of primitive Christian faith. For them, as for Paul, Jesus Christ is the glorified heavenly Lord, the Savior, dead and risen. Nevertheless, a man such as Mark was closer to the original soil of the gospel than the apostle to the Gentiles. He was in the midst of the stream of the living tradition of Jesus. In this milieu the Lord's words and deeds had incomparable religious value. They were a foundation of the common life. Mark was so rooted in this environment that there is scarcely a trace of Pauline dogmatic in his Gospel (cf. M. Werner, *Der Einfluss paulinischer Theologie im Markusevangelium,* Giessen, 1923). He still lives in the sacred recollections with an artlessness which did not take offence at all the concrete and human features of the narratives about Jesus. It is not the same with Matthew and Luke. The universal and transcendent viewpoint common to Mark, Paul, and primitive Christianity in general does not show itself in a species of arrangement of the naive, popular tradition, but in a work of *redaction,* in the general organization of the Gospel text, in the composition and remarks which frame and group what is transmitted.

The result for our method is that we must accurately distinguish between the *popular elements* of the tradition and those which are a later *redaction.* This is the principle to guide us when we examine the question of chief interest to us here. In effect, redactional elements are of special importance for our question, because, directly or indirectly, they express the overall evaluation of the oldest Christian era on the thaumaturgy of Jesus. On the other hand, where their genuineness is involved, the miracle stories reflect a popular faith, naive and bereft of reflection, and do not tell us what we want to know, viz., how the Christian mission treated the miracles of Jesus in its preaching and teaching.

In this regard, whatever viewpoints we find in the synoptic Gospels, we will look for in the *Acts of the Apostles* as well. If we find the same conception of Jesus' miracles in these two areas, we can flatly state what the primitive Christian mission thought and said of them.

First we will examine the role which miracle as such played in this mission.

MIRACLE IN THE CHRISTIAN MISSION

Close connection with miracle distinguished the primitive Christian mission from the Jewish mission and the propaganda of philosophic popularization. In Paul, the greatest Christian missionary of this period, we repeatedly encounter utterances indicating he was quite familiar with the miracles accompanying the missionary task and that he performed some himself. He writes in 1 Thess. 1:5: "for our Gospel came to you not only in word, but also in *power* (ἐν δυνάμει) and in the Holy Spirit and with full conviction. . . ." Reflecting on his activity and speaking of what Christ has done through him, he says in Rom. 15:19: λόγῳ καὶ ἔργῳ, ἐν δυνάμει σημείων καὶ τεράτων, ἐν δυνάμει πνεύματος θεοῦ, ὥστε με ἀπὸ Ἰερουσαλὴμ . . . πεπληρωκέναι τὸ εὐαγγέλιον τοῦ Χριστοῦ. When he defends his own cause in 2 Corinthians, he declares that he was in no way inferior to the "superlative" apostles: "The σημεῖα of a true apostle were performed among you in all patience, with signs, and wonders, and mighty works" (12:12).

Paul here is a witness to the missionary practice of primitive Christianity. From the outset, the gospel was presented amid awe-inspiring wonders. This is excellently formulated in Heb. 2:4: Salvation was at first declared by the Lord and confirmed by those who heard him, "while God also bore witness by signs and wonders and various miracles and by gifts of the Holy Spirit distributed according to his own will." Similarly, the inauthentic conclusion of Mark (16:17) enumerates the σημεῖα to accompany those who will have believed: They will drive out demons in Jesus' name; they will take serpents in their hands, and they will drink any deadly beverage without harm; they will lay their hands on the sick and they will be healed. "And they went forth, and preached everywhere, while the Lord worked with them and confirmed the message by the signs that attended it."

The book of the *Acts of the Apostles* completes this general characterization by furnishing vivid examples which, at exactly this juncture and aside from their documentary value, have great importance because they are typical. In the *apocryphal* Acts of the Apostles this feature is of course pushed to the extreme.

The close bond between oldest Christian propaganda and miracle is a fact of extreme importance. It corresponds to the enthusiastic and inspired character of the epoch. This special character poses an important problem for us, and its solution greatly affects our historical understanding of the origins of our religion. In order to explain the miracles in primitive Christian mission, it is not enough to draw attention to similar phenomena in the religions of Hellenism and Judaism. Certainly, the thaumaturgy of popular religion to a great extent lived on in the churches in Christian form and widely influenced ancient traditions. But this would not explain the rapid spread of this practice in the primitive church. We should rather note the fact that in general the miraculous element exists with the origin of the church. The visions of Christ, the resurrection appearances, created an enthusiastic and steadfast faith; the supernatural irresistibly imposed itself on the disciples and produced a state of mind which reveled in miracle. After all, the decisive miracle was imminent—the immediate transformation of all things after brief delay, and with the parousia of the risen and glorified Lord the total victory of the celestial powers. To explain these facts we must not forget one essential point— the extremely vivid recollection of Jesus' miracles. His disciples and servants after him merely continued them in his name. In them, his action was prolonged. Thus a thaumaturgy immediately took shape which served as a norm for mission and which continued to develop under various environmental influences. The Gospels relate that when Jesus first sent out his disciples, he gave them power over demons (Mark 6:7ff.). That this feature is viewed as a later stylizing is no less proof that a line is deliberately pursued here of which Jesus is the point of departure.

How were these phenomena reflected in the very consciousness of primitive Christianity? It is evident that the eminently religious temper of the period has one of its principal sources in these dynamic experiences. The miraculous formed and dominated the general conception of the world. We may call this conception primitive since it includes the typical features of a popular view of reality. Rationalism is totally absent from it and it exhibits a naive sense for the supernatural which manifests itself constantly, but in various ways. This ancient and popular conception assumed a special form in primitive Christianity: people believed they were living at the end of time. Salvation is a miracle beginning with the incarnation and resurrection of the Son of God and ending in the transformation of all things at the end of time. Thus the miracle of redemption embraces all of life, the physical as well as the moral. It follows that the transcendent forces are always and continually manifest in the marvelous events and the wonders of the servants of God.

The apostle Paul completely shares this view. For him, Christ's resurrection and parousia give the framework of the present era; he awaits the instantaneous transformation of the living and the resurrection of the dead (1 Cor. 15; 1 Thess. 4), and he describes the desire of all creation to be finally freed (Rom. 8). But even now the divine power erupts in our world by spreading and renewing life. To the λόγος, the ἔργον (Rom. 15:18) is invariably joined in missionary activity. The Spirit at work in the church manifests himself by an abundance of *charismata* (1 Cor. 12 and 14). Paul himself has direct relation to God through revelations (Gal. 2:2) and visions (1 Cor. 9:1; 15:8; 2 Cor. 12). Here too, the apostle's vigorous originality clearly stood out. For him the greatest miracle is God's love for fallen and perverted humanity, and the term *dynamis* which always denotes this miracle [7] furnishes succinct definition to the gospel (Rom. 1:16). Love and edification are the higher principle to which life in the churches must be subordinated (1 Cor. 8 and 13), and the fruits of the Spirit are, above all, Christian virtues (Gal. 5:22). If he himself is weak and tormented by the devil, the grace of the Lord is sufficient for him (2 Cor. 12:7ff.). But what we must chiefly consider here is what binds him to the general conceptions of primitive Christianity.

As to miracles which serve missionary propaganda, we encounter in Paul a terminology which is already fixed and, compared to that of Acts, turns out to be current in apostolic times.[8] The fundamental idea is the same—the miracles manifest that divine power which sustains the mission, acts through it, and has created all things new in the ethical and material realms. The missionary is the intermediary whom God uses in order to act (cf. the typical expression in Rom. 15:18 [ἃ] κατειργάσατο Χριστὸς δι' ἐμοῦ εἰς ὑπακοὴν ἐθνῶν. . . .). If this is the main and higher point of view, a slight shift follows naturally and spontaneously—miracle serves to *legitimate* God's messenger and his preaching. We recall the word of Paul already cited from 2 Cor.

12:12 (τὰ σημεῖα τοῦ ἀποστόλου), and the passage in 1 Cor. 2:4: "my message did not consist ἐν πειθοῖ σοφίας but ἐν ἀποδείξει πνεύματος καὶ δυνάμεως"; then Heb. 2:4: συνεπιμαρτυροῦντος θεοῦ σημείοις κτλ. Both viewpoints are joined in Mark 16:20: τοῦ κυρίου συνεργοῦντος καὶ τὸν λόγον βεβαιοῦντος διὰ τῶν ἐπακολουθούντων σημείων.

The missionary in both cases is the instrument of the divine and mediator of the divine message. But popular mentality loved to see in supernatural power a personal attribute of the apostle; with astonishment and respect homage was paid the power of the thaumaturge. Thus a Christian aretalogy emerged which developed largely in the legends of apostles and saints.

The canonical book of Acts still remains at such a level that the miraculous is subordinated to the great religious purpose. Purely aretalogical features are very rarely encountered there. Ed. Meyer *(Ursprung und Anfänge* III, pp. 5ff., 16) is certainly right when he protests against the title later given this work (Πράξεις ἀποστόλων, i.e. the miracles of the apostles).[9] However varied, even offensive the miracles of the Acts might be, the narrative is still far from disappearing in the miraculous. What dominates is the basic religious thought of spreading salvation. This is all the more remarkable since several of the narratives in Acts recount miracles which originally were told only for the miracle's sake. The *auctor ad Theophilum* subordinated them to a superior view: they must accent the great purpose of his work, viz., to further the triumphal and irresistible march of the gospel. Cases are rare where aretalogical and popular interest prevails, so that miracle serves directly and particularly to glorify the hero, as e.g. in the narrative of Paul's being bitten by a serpent (28:1ff.) ; in that of Eutychus who was raised from death at Troas (20:7ff.), or in those relating that the shadow or clothing of the apostles healed the sick (5:15; 19:11ff.).

We may assume that this fine religious tact in regard to miracle is found with most of the eminent personalities of the ancient church. For all its enthusiasm, primitive Christianity had a very sure sense of the fundamentally moral character of religion. This sense was still developing powerfully under Old Testament influence. Later, we will see how the defenders of this moral conscience contended with the miracle mania which threatened to engulf everything, and what sort of arguments they used. Subsequently—and this too was a precious heritage of the ancient people of God—the still strong sense of the insuperable distance between God and man opposed any divinization of man. The story reported in Acts 14:8ff. is significant in this regard. It relates that at Lystra the apostles indignantly refused the divine honors offered them.

In addition, we must mention an important factor which will concern us in the following pages—thaumaturgy in the Christian church menaced the gospel's prestige in the eyes of its contemporaries. Alongside Christian thaumaturges were others who did not always enjoy the best reputation. In this period, magicians, sorcerers and charlatans were very numerous. It would have been fatal to confuse the Christian missionary with such a group. The greatest precautions were taken against them. This is clearly stated in the Book of Acts. Peter, after having healed the paralytic beggar, says to the startled crowd: "Men of Israel, why do you wonder at this, or why do you stare at us, as though by our own power or piety we had made him walk? The God of Abraham and of Isaac and of Jacob, the God of our fathers, glorified his servant Jesus" (3:12). These words must not only prepare for the message about Jesus, but also prevent a malevolent interpretation of miracle. When we are told of the apostles' encounter with the great magicians Simon Magus and Elymas (Chaps. 8 and 13), it is to prove there is no connection between them and the Christian missionaries. On the contrary, they are bitter adversaries. The name and spirit of Jesus are beyond all magic (cf. Acts 19:19, the story of the magical books burned at Ephesus).[10]

We will see that traces of this tendency already appear in the Gospel tradition, and that miracle as such was one of the first problems primitive Christianity had to solve. Still, we must first briefly sketch the leading ideas applied to the thaumaturgy accompanying the preaching of Jesus.

THE MIRACLES OF JESUS IN PRIMITIVE CHRISTIAN PREACHING AND TEACHING

What did the missionaries of primitive Christianity think of the miracles of Jesus? They proclaimed the Son of God, Jesus Christ, his incarnation, crucifixion, and resurrection by accenting the decisive moments of the history of salvation. They naturally had to take into account the life of Jesus, with an

eye to the tradition which recounted his activity
and from the beginning formed an integral part of
missionary preaching. But there were also internal
reasons. When addressed to Jews, preaching had to
demonstrate that Jesus was the Messiah predicted
by the Old Testament and that he accordingly fulfilled the prophecies. It was then necessary to prove
his activity had truly messianic character. Finally,
the missionaries had to surmount the scandal of the
cross by demonstrating that Jesus' death had not
been deserved but was, on the contrary, an abominable crime committed by his judges.

For the heathen, it was also necessary to depict
the σώτηρ become flesh, his life and work. To discover
the unity of his personality through the various
phases of his existence was a preoccupation answer-
ing to a religious need.[11]

In both instances, the point of view was transcendental. But, according to circumstances, intent
and interpretation doubtless produced characteristic
differences in the manner of depicting the historical
events and setting them off to advantage.

In what light was Jesus' thaumaturgy presented
in missionary preaching?

We have already underscored the fact that Paul
never mentions Jesus' miracles; in general the apostle says almost nothing of Jesus' activity. If, on the
other hand, we consult the Book of Acts, we derive
certain hints, chiefly from two passages in the missionary discourses of Peter.

In his sermon on the day of Pentecost, the apostle
declares: "Jesus of Nazareth, a man attested to you
by God with mighty works and wonders and signs

which God did through him in your midst, as you yourselves know, this Jesus . . . you crucified and killed by the hands of lawless men" (2:22).

In the house of Cornelius, Peter utters these words: "You know . . . how God anointed Jesus of Nazareth with the Holy Spirit and with power; how he went about doing good (εὐεργετῶν) and healing all that were oppressed by the devil, for God was with him. . . . They put him to death by hanging him on a tree" (10:38).

In the first case, the *dynameis* of Jesus attest to his divine mission which brings to light the contradictory attitude of the Jews. The one to whom God himself bore witness they crucified—this is the dreadful revolt against God himself. The second passage describes Jesus as benefactor (εὐεργέτης), as devoted and kind Savior of the unfortunate. But the cruelest ingratitude was his payment.

We see then that Jesus' thaumaturgy was considered from two points of view, viz., as a divine witness and as a εὐεργετεῖν. It is no accident that we find the first of these in a discourse to the Jews, whereas the second is addressed to the Roman centurion. In Luke's case the two points of view, the Jewish and Greek elements, are combined. The ἀπόδειξις motif had been given him by the tradition; but we will hardly be mistaken in assuming that he had marked preference for the εὐεργέτης motif. Indeed, there is complete and indisputable agreement that sentiment holds a much greater place in the third Gospel than in the other two synoptics. Here Jesus is readily depicted with the features of a benevolent physician of body and soul, the Savior

of sins, who aids us in our distress. Finally, he is
the true εὐεργέτης, contrasted with other benefactors
to whom this noble title is ordinarily assigned (Luke
22:25). This is already manifest in Jesus' first discourse at Nazareth (4:16ff.), where he applies to
himself the lofty words uttered by Isaiah (61:1ff.).
Luke's style is generally distinguished by a certain
sensitivity, but we do not wish to stress that here.
We note only the touching scene where Jesus returns the son to his grief-stricken mother (7:11-
17).

Underlining the εὐεργέτης motif in this fashion,
Luke no doubt merely follows the natural bent of his
sensitivity and thought. This type of outlook, however, has some degree of support in the tradition at
the base of Luke's narrative. On numerous occasions, Mark already accented the compassion of
Jesus (1:41; 6:34; 8:2: σπλαγχνισθείς). But it is especially Jesus' *death* which assumes the character of
an act of redeeming love and service (Mark 10:45).
Luke's basic conception and his narrative style were
undoubtedly developed in a milieu which cultivated
the mystical sense. The divine absorbs the human,
purifies it and confers on it a divine power. There
we are certainly in the presence of Hellenistic and
Greek influences. The benefactor who went from
place to place (διῆλθεν εὐεργετῶν, Acts 10:38) and by
his teaching freed hearts from passion and error,
and by his supernatural power reestablished the
harmony of human nature ruined by sin and dis-
ease, was a popular figure in the literature of the
period.[12] Given this framework, Luke has revived it
and filled it with the tradition about Jesus. But an

inverse reaction also occurs—this scheme gave the tradition a particular nuance. The dual aspect of the activity of the εὐεργέτης requires the dual perspective of the *dicta* and *facta* from which Luke views the life of Jesus (Acts 1:1: ποιεῖν τε καὶ διδάσκειν; cf. Papias in Eusebius' *Ecclesiastical History* III, 39, 15: τὰ ὑπὸ τοῦ κυρίου ἢ λεχθέντα ἢ πραχθέντα). In Luke 1:1, the term πράγματα sums up everything.

In Luke's principal source, i.e. the *Gospel of Mark*, the ἀπόδειξις motif is not immediately and clearly evident. Nevertheless, it dominates the entire account. If it is not apparent nor expressly formulated, it is sufficiently explained by the idea the evangelist develops of Jesus' activity in his contact with the public.

In 1:4-39, the evangelist describes Jesus' activity, indicating the characteristic traits of his ministry as he understands it. With his messianic vocation, Jesus receives the Spirit of God (1:10ff.); then he leaves obscurity to preach repentance and the gospel of the kingdom (1:14ff.); he calls his disciples (1:16-20); teaches the people (1:21ff.); drives out a demon (1:22-28); heals Peter's mother-in-law and many other sick and demoniacs (1:32ff.). Verse 39 sums up this activity: "And he went throughout all Galilee, preaching in their synagogues and casting out demons."

What Mark himself thought of Jesus' activity is disclosed in the words of the astonished crowd: "What is this? A new teaching! With authority he commands even the unclean spirits, and they obey him" (1:27). It is his ἐξουσία which is manifest in his teaching as well as in his *dynameis* (cf. 2:10).

In this way also the ἀπόδειξις motif is expressed in this passage. But what strikes us is that the people who utter these words we are quoting do not understand their full significance. They do not draw the obvious conclusion from the facts. They take Jesus to be a great prophet (8:28), but do not discover in him the Messiah, the Son of God.

The crowd could not—its mind was blind and deaf. Even the disciples often did not understand (πώρωσις in 6:52 and 8:17). Still, they ended by seeing in Jesus the Messiah (8:29). Mark certainly considers this discovery a miracle, a divine revelation (cf. also Matt. 16:17: ἀποκάλυψις)—analogous to the daily experience of the Christian mission that some accept the faith whereas most refuse to accept the truth.

In a word, Jesus acts and speaks in his capacity as Messiah of God without being recognized as such. This formula explains the conception of Jesus' activity in the oldest Gospel. The narrative of Jesus' entry into Jerusalem is instructive in this regard (11:7-10). The entry has a totally messianic character. Jesus makes entry into the city of David, according to the prophecy (which though not expressly mentioned is nevertheless assumed), sitting on an ass's foal. But the joyous praises of the crowd are *not addressed to the Messiah,* but to the *famous prophet and thaumaturge.* His arrival for the great feast rouses enthusiasm and makes hosannas ring. The words, εὐλογημένος ὁ ἐρχόμενος ἐν ὀνόματι κυρίου are a liturgical formula, a greeting normally given pilgrims. And the acclamations with which they hailed "the reign which comes from David, our Father," prove only that the presence of the great Galilean rabbi released patriotic and eschatological enthusiasm. But the crowd is unaware that he is the king of this reign so ardently desired.[13]

From this angle, Mark views the tradition. He neither created nor greatly retouched it—it was given to him. But he could only explain the attitude of the people and its leaders by drastically underlining their manifest insensitivity to spiritual things. This explanation is not his own, but was commonly adopted in primitive Christianity, as we learn from Paul and Acts (cf. the notion of ἄγνοια in 3:17; 13:27). Thus one by one the props of Wrede's thesis of the "messianic secret" fall away. According to this theory, Mark retouched and messianized the narratives of Jesus' activity in conformity with a loftier notion of the Messiah. But then he must explain why the people did not recognize Jesus as Messiah, and Mark replies: because he hid his messianic character. But this is not correct. Actually, Mark received a tradition presenting Jesus as speaking and acting in his capacity as Son of God full of power. If the people did not hail the Messiah in him, Mark together with many of his coreligionists believed that their ability to perceive spiritual things was perverted.

So we have a right to speak of a "messianic secret" in Mark, but not in *Wrede's* sense. There is something mysterious and deeply moving in this declaration that Jesus is the Messiah and that he manifests himself as such without anyone's suspecting his sacred presence. No doubt, Mark has acutely sensed the special charm, at once romantic and disturbing, emanating from this idea. But there is more. According to him, Jesus draws certain conclusions from this indifference of the people, first of all, by giving esoteric character to his teaching about the kingdom of God. It is given only to disciples to know the μυστήρια τῆς βασιλείας τοῦ θεοῦ (4:11-34) ; the others are οἱ ἔξω (4:11; cf. 1 Thess. 4:12), to whom he directs the word only in parabolic form (4:33ff.).[14] This declaration helps us to understand the other passages which tell that Jesus forbade the direct revelation of himself as Messiah (8:30; 9:9). If men were actually so deaf and blind they did not perceive spiritual things, the principal secret of the kingdom of God had to be reserved for the small number to whom it should be communicated. This attitude results naturally from the overall conception. It cannot be maintained that Mark intended to hide Jesus' messianic character at all costs. If the great truths of the kingdom of God must remain μυστήρια, it follows necessarily from the peoples' state of mind; it is something of a chastisement.[15]

Hence, in the Gospel of Mark Jesus is the Son of God who speaks and acts as Messiah but is not understood and consequently remains a μυστήριον. He speaks to οἱ ἔξω in the form of parables. All his activity, we could say, is nothing but a single παραβολή, whose true and inner meaning is accessible only to the initiated. Like the Gospel of John, many of the utterances in Mark have a dual meaning and produce, so to speak, a double sound (cf. the significant term ὁ ἐρχόμενος in 11:9) ; some day an attempt at a systematic explanation of the entire Gospel must be made from this special point of view.

We will be very brief on Matthew. He has not consciously appropriated the viewpoint of the Markan "messianic secret," whose significance we have specified. Matthew puts the principal stress on Jesus' teaching which he considers the fulfillment of divine revelation recorded in Scripture. Jesus teaches the emerging church (16:18) the new and better righteousness (5:17-20). Given this intellectual orientation, Matthew is little interested in the historical aspect of Jesus' personality and the people's judgment on it. Utterances concerning the μυστήρια of the heavenly kingdom which Matthew borrows from Mark and paraphrases (13:10-17), do not spell the solution to some serious problem. This is why the ἀπόδειξις motif appears with so much ingenuity in Matthew. From the moment Jesus walked on the sea, the disciples gave him homage as "Son of God" (14:33).

Besides the ἀπόδειξις, we find in Matthew, a scribe, the idea of prophecy fulfilled. He also applies this idea to the miracles (11:4). If we are sometimes reminded of the εὐεργέτης motif in Luke, we still cannot claim the points of view are identical. Jesus' miracles are inspired by the same love as his sufferings and death, cf. 8:17: Jesus heals the sick and the demoniacs "to fulfill what was spoken by the prophet Isaiah: 'he took our infirmities and bore our diseases.' " In general, Matthew seems to have viewed the activity of the Savior Jesus against the background of Deutero-Isaiah, cf. 12:15-20. As soon as he establishes a parallel between Jesus' miracles and the figure of the Servant of God, he must con-

sider miracle as flowing from the love which makes
itself the servant and support of all.[16]

JESUS' WORDS CONCERNING MIRACLE

How did Jesus himself conceive his activity as
thaumaturge; how did he regard his healings and
his victories over demons?[17] To this question, which
we only intend to touch lightly here, we can only
reply with conjecture. What took place in the depths
of Jesus' soul will always remain a mystery no
source will be able to uncover. All we can know are
the essential elements of his message, some examples of the *dynameis* he performed and some rare
utterances connected with miracle. We may draw
certain conclusions, nothing more. Whoever believes
he can define Jesus' consciousness in all its vast
richness on the basis of a few generalities is greatly
mistaken, and proves he has not really been touched
by the originality, penetrating psychology, and im-
measurable depth of his personality.

Yet we can risk some remarks without commit-
ting ourselves. Jesus preached the gospel of the
kingdom of heaven: πεπλήρωται ὁ καιρὸς καὶ ἤγγικεν ἡ
βασιλεία τοῦ θεοῦ—exactly as Mark, for good reason,
characterizes Jesus' message (1:15). The presence
in him of the gift of healing and exorcism was undoubtedly interpreted as one of the signs preceding
the coming of the kingdom of heaven. In its own
way, this reign was an essentially miraculous act.
The great cataclysm and the new creation will suddenly arrive, and the new world will be completely
filled with divine power and joy. All the evils and

infirmities of this age will be abolished and healed at a single stroke.

This was certainly Jesus' controlling conviction in his activity as thaumaturge. His *dynameis* are the effects of his mighty eschatological faith which in turn was anchored in his unshakable faith in God and totally filled and gladdened him. Everywhere and always he sought to discern the signs preceding the coming of the kingdom. But he also sensed that by his activity he was himself effectively contributing to its coming. He was creating the future by his wonders; the forces of the world to come were already being manifested in and by him.

It is thus false to view Jesus' thaumaturgy only from a humanitarian and sentimental point of view. This activity was rather an integral element in his messianic work, an anticipation of the great and wondrous future and a way of bringing it about. Naturally, this attitude did not exclude the concern Jesus felt for the unfortunate and the wretched whom he met on his way. On the contrary, this fact we must acknowledge to a great extent when referring back to the oldest tradition which already spoke of the *compassion* of Jesus. But it is precisely to understand this oldest tradition that we must always have before our eyes the messianic character of Jesus' miracles. Then we will have a solid point of support for puzzling out Jesus' own evaluation of this part of his activity.

The few *utterances* of Jesus concerning the miracles transmitted by the synoptic tradition do not lead us beyond this general observation. If we examine the passages which occur in this connection,

we will see immediately that we must divide them
into two groups: first, the utterances which have a
polemical and *apologetic* tone, then those concerning
miracles and *faith,* which raise a question of principle.

POLEMIC AND APOLOGETIC SPEECHES

First, a word about the *exorcisms* referred to in
Matt. 12:27ff. and Luke 11:19ff. Later, we will examine this speech in its proper context. We believe
it has been attached as an afterthought to the speech
which immediately precedes it. Some redactor could
not allow that Jesus was content to reply to the
Pharisees' question by remaining on the defensive:
"And if I cast out demons by Beelzebul, by whom
do your sons cast them out?" This is just a retort,
and, as such, it is negative. This redactor also
felt compelled to formulate a positive conclusion
resulting from the contrast with the ἐν Βεελζεβούλ:
"But if it is *by the finger (Spirit) of God* that I
cast out demons, then the kingdom of God has come
upon you." This conclusion expresses the thought of
the primitive church, but no doubt also gives that of
Jesus himself. The struggle against Satan is already
at its peak; Jesus everywhere puts his servants to
flight. With bold anticipation, Jesus could already
exclaim: ἔφθασεν ἐφ' ὑμᾶς ἡ βασιλεία τοῦ θεοῦ. From the
church's point of view, this speech is most characteristic. It shows what great importance the oldest
era assigned the exorcisms. They are one of the
characteristic signs of the kingdom of God. The
flight of unclean spirits from Christian exorcists

was not the least indication of the presence of the Spirit of God.[18]

As to the form of the logion, ἡ βασιλεία τοῦ θεοῦ would have been immediately suggested by its contrast with ἡ βασιλεία αὐτοῦ (τοῦ Σατανᾶ) which precedes. All things considered, the author of this speech is thinking of the church in the heart of which *dynameis,* divine forces, are manifest and which, by its cultus, forms a single spirit with the Messiah from now on.

The unrepentant cities in Matt. 11:20-24; Luke 10:13-15. The woes addressed to Chorazin, Bethsaida, and Capernaum very much call to mind the speeches of Matt. 12:41ff. and Luke 11:13ff. In both instances, pagans and pagan cities are given as an example to Israel, to its own shame. And it is said that on the day of judgment their inhabitants who do not form part of the chosen people will be dealt with less rigorously than Israel. From the point of view of form as well, the resemblance is quite marked. The two groups of speeches exhibit a strictly uniform structure, and the final phrase is repeated as a refrain: ἀνεκτότερον ἔσται . . . , Matt. 11:22-42; ἰδοὺ πλεῖον Ἰωνᾶ (Σολωμῶνος) ὧδε, 12:41f. Here we undoubtedly have an outline of primitive Christian polemic in a gnomic and stylized form. We see this polemic scheme applied to the two aspects of Jesus' activity—his preaching and teaching (wisdom; Matt. 12) and his *dynameis* (Matt. 11). In the latter case it was necessary that the example of foreigners who were to fill Israel with shame take hypothetical form: εἰ ἐγένοντο (11:21). This application set the ἀπόδειξις motif in bold relief.

Precisely these cities, which witnessed nearly all Jesus' wonders, should have recognized in him the Messiah of God and heard his preaching of repentance. For the rest, it is not a question of faith here, but of repentance, and this is characteristic. Μετάνοια is the first commandment of missionary preaching. Perhaps we must also note some influence of the story of the prophet Jonah, the prototype of Jesus (cf. 12:41: "for they repented at the preaching of Jonah").

The refusal to give a sign from heaven, in Mark 8:11-12; Matt. 16:1-4; 12:38-42 and Luke 11:29-32. Mark and the speech source (Q) transmit a word of Jesus refusing his adversaries' demand for a σημεῖον ἐξ οὐρανοῦ. In Q, we note an amplification under the influence of Christian scribes—this generation will not be given a miracle other than Jonah's.[19] In Mark we read these simple categorical words: "Why does this generation seek a sign? Truly, I say to you, no sign shall be given to this generation." The question as to whether this tradition reproduces an episode in the life of Jesus or is of later origin does not concern us here. What interests us is the importance of this word for the church. Here we find a very distinct echo of believers' debates with enemies of the faith concerning Jesus' miracles. The adversaries do not want to admit that the miracles are a messianic ἀπόδειξις. The *dynameis* assigned to Jesus would not be able to prove his divine mission. For this, there would have to be a particular σημεῖον ἐξ οὐρανοῦ. From the church's point of view, this objection could only be considered proof of the adversaries' obduracy and ill-will. And

the word, "no σημεῖον will be given this generation,"
seemed an obvious confirmation of this judgment.
This categorical refusal implies both judgment and
threat—"let the unbelievers be given over to their
blindness!" One thing ought to be noted. In Mark
8:11, the miracle demanded of Jesus is considered
a "proof," which indicates an openly hostile intent
(πειράζοντες αὐτόν, cf. 10:2; 12:15). The Pharisees are
at work here, the murderers of the Lord, the persecutors of the faithful. These men are prey not only
to their unrepentance and spiritual blindness as are
the people, but also to a violent animosity and a
merciless hate. They seek out any opportunity to set
traps for the Christians. Their demand for miracle
does not arise from their love of truth, but from
consummate treachery. Though there may be an
allusion to the leaders of the Jewish people here,
Jesus' reply nevertheless refers in a general way to
"this generation." The Jews, of course, are judged
and characterized according to their leaders. This
was commonly done in primitive Christianity and
the Christian church (cf. οἱ Ἰουδαῖοι in the Fourth
Gospel, and in Paul, e.g. in 1 Thess. 2:14ff.; 1 Cor.
1:22; Rom. Chaps. 9ff.).[20]

MIRACLES AND FAITH

Faith is the condition naturally required of the
one wishing to be healed by Jesus' supernatural
power. Whoever confidently appeals to him in his
distress is helped. Healing is the response to the
confidence of the sick person, to his "faith" (ἡ πίστις
σου σέσωκέν σε in Mark 5:34; 10:52). We need not

consider any mystical connection between faith and healing. Faith is the tribute due to the great prophet, an homage which is graciously rewarded. This is clear from the passage in Mark 1:40, where the leper says to Jesus: "If you will, you can make me clean." Jesus answers him with these words full of majesty: "I will; be clean." This same sublime goodness toward him who confidently seeks his aid is expressed in the formula "be it done for you as you have believed" (Matt. 8:13; 15:28). It is also demonstrated in certain instances where the healing does not occur on account of the faith of the diseased himself, but on account of others' faith (the centurion's servant in Matt. 8; the daughter of the Syro-Phoenician woman in Matt. 15). In the narrative of the paralytic at Capernaum we read, ἰδὼν αὐτῶν τὴν πίστιν (Mark 2:5), that is, the faith of those who carried the bed.

Taken in this completely natural sense, "faith" is the condition for miracle. It is a fact that Jesus exercised his supernatural power only when his help was requested or sought after. Faith could be "great," i.e., perfectly conscious and without inhibitions (the centurion), or even quite bold (the Syro-Phoenician woman). But faith can also take the form of a simple request or popular demand—Jesus' aid is always the response to an expressly formulated or tacit prayer which presupposes "faith." This is also the case in the healing of the woman afflicted with the issue of blood (Mark 5:34). The healing occurs in magical fashion with the touching of Jesus' garments ("a power had gone forth from him"), but it is faith which prompts the woman to touch them.

In general, the synoptic tradition maintains this point of view. Jesus only rarely makes use of his supernatural power when the diseased or his parents do not request it. With regard to the demoniacs, this variable rarely comes into play, which explains why Jesus takes the offensive against Satan as soon as the occasion arises. Where the healing provokes debate with adversaries, interest fastens on the debate, and it is not expressly stated that help was asked for the sick person (e.g., Mark 3:1-6). With regard to the healing of Peter's mother-in-law, special request for help was obviated by the particularly close connections with this family. The raising of the young man of Nain is only found in Luke, who readily depicts Jesus as the merciful benefactor. Jesus intervenes and raises even the dead, when his heart is moved by compassion.[21]

It is apparent that the entire synoptic tradition assumes that Jesus has unlimited supernatural power. The continual correlation between healing and faith gives all the more witness to the religious tact of this tradition. But it would be an error to believe we could find in a single passage the idea that in the exercise of his supernatural power Jesus was bound to the faith of men. The celebrated narrative of the unbelief which Jesus encountered at Nazareth in no way weakens this truth. Mark 6:5ff. relates Jesus' visit to Nazareth, his native city. "And he could do no mighty work there, except that he laid his hands upon a few sick people and healed them. And he marveled because of their unbelief."

The severe reprimand contained in this word, directed to the unbelief of the people of Nazareth, is usually not seen. Still, its meaning is unquestionable—the magnitude of unbelief is shown in the fact that Jesus was "able" to perform only a few healings, which means his help was not sought after, and this to the shame of Jesus' native city. He would have been able to perform miracles if the opportunity had been given him. This explains the οὐκ ἐδύνατο.[22]

The correlation between faith and miracle is hence completely natural. Whoever wishes to find help from the thaumaturge must ask it of him, which again presupposes faith. But in the synoptics we already see a reflection upon this correlation of miracle and faith. Both factors were considered in their inner, as it were metaphysical, relationship.

A similar, but not identical reflection is found in Matt. 9:27-31, where Jesus addresses the two blind men with the question, "do you believe that I am able to do this?" They answer, "yes, Lord," and he heals them saying, "according to your faith be it done to you." Here we see a trace of the thaumaturgy which Matthew uses to fill the framework of this pericope. It is a matter of strengthening the conscience, will, and confidence of the diseased, of creating the kind of psychic conditions favorable to the healing. The same is true of Matt. 20:32: "What do you want me to do for you?" as well as of Acts 3:4 βλέψον εἰς ἡμᾶς and Mark 5:36: μὴ φοβοῦ, μόνον πίστευε. . . . But practice is changed upon reflection. Born of experience, reflection of this type shaped the story of the healing of the epileptic in Mark

9:14-29. In the way in which it is preserved to us, this pericope has its decisive point in the question, "Why could we not cast it [the demon] out?" (vs. 28; cf. vs. 18). The answer is indirectly given in vs. 19: ὦ γενεὰ ἄπιστος—because of the disciples' unbelief. Verse 23 abounds with this meaning: "All things are possible to him who believes." This word, of course, has Christian exorcists in mind. But the redactor had difficulty inserting this maxim into the whole of the narrative and was not very successful in his attempt for he makes the father say to Jesus, "if you can do anything, have pity on us and help us." Jesus answers him, "if you can! All things are possible to him who believes." This would make it appear that Jesus worked miracles because of his *own* faith, which the redactor certainly neither thought nor meant to say. In reality, this word is addressed to the disciples. When the father cries out, "Lord, I believe, help my unbelief," we no doubt have the sigh of the Christian exorcist who senses his powerlessness. In the mouth of the father, this word is deprived of meaning because, given the situation, it is not a question of his faith. Another feature of the narrative proves the accuracy of our observation. When the disciples then ask Jesus why they could not heal the boy, we should expect them to receive this response: "It is because of your unbelief" (the reply given, in effect, in Matt. 17:20). But instead, Jesus, according to Mark, indicates how weak faith can become stronger and recover its supernatural power by means of prayer (Mark 9:29). There is no doubt that the Christian exorcist is speaking of his experience here. Most manuscripts still add fasting to faith (προσευχῇ καὶ νηστείᾳ). Prayer and fasting are the most powerful means for giving focus to the religious consciousness and heightening the inner powers.

Πίστις and πιστεύειν have a wholly technical meaning here. It is a matter of faith which produces miracles. Concerning this faith, another utterance of Jesus has been preserved in Mark 11:22ff., and Matt. 21:21ff.: "Have faith in God. Truly, I say to you, whoever says to this mountain, 'Be taken up and cast into the sea,' and does not doubt in his heart, but believes that what he says will come to pass, it will be done for him. There I tell you, whatever you ask in prayer, believe that you receive it, and you will." The speech source (Q) also reproduces this logion (Matt. 17:20; Luke 17:6), but in a different form: "For truly, I say to you, if you have faith as a grain of mustard seed, you will say to this mountain, 'move hence to yonder place,' and it will move; and nothing will be impossible to you" (in Luke: "if you had faith as a grain of mustard seed, you could say to this sycamine tree, 'Be rooted up, and be planted in the sea,' and it would obey you"). Luke's version is obviously secondary. 1 Cor. 13:2 provides one more argument in support of this observation. The final words of Matthew's text, "and nothing will be impossible to you," were added later. By comparing Mark's text with the two from Q, we are immediately struck by a significant difference. In Q, this speech is a maxim whose paradoxical character has been pushed to the limit. Mark, on the other hand, gives *instruction*. In Q the contrast between the tiny mustard seed and the great mountain immediately recalls the other image of the camel and the needle's eye. We note here Jesus' characteristic use of extreme hyperbole. Mark, however, contrasts the notion of πιστεύειν with διακρίνεσθαι, as can also be observed in James 1:6.

Jesus teaches that man ought always have absolute confidence in God. This confidence is the spiritual sphere in which man ought to live (Matt. 6:24ff.). In critical situations, in times of anguish and despondency, he reproaches his disciples for their lack of faith and unbelief (Mark 4:40). Such is the speech of the faith which moves mountains; it is a speech of reproof. Matthew interpreted it as a reproach, evidenced by the place he gave it at the end of the pericope on the healing of the epileptic boy (17:20). But he also set it in a certain relation to *miracle*. This was not, however, the original intention of the speech. In uttering it, Jesus did not especially have miracle in mind. In the boldly paradoxical form it assumes, it signifies that the inner attitude of faith can, without any outward expression, overcome the most difficult and crushing circumstances. Later, it was believed that πίστις had a kind of magical connotation, denoting a faith which produces miracles, and the speech was stripped of its paradoxical form by transforming it into a practical instruction. Significantly, Mark combined it with the word concerning prayer offered in faith.[23]

We are then at the very center of the missionary and ecclesiastical life of primitive Christianity. Among the gifts of the Spirit which should be operative in the church, Paul mentions πίστις in 1 Cor. 12:9; cf. 13:2. It is something other than the Christian faith which gives salvation. It is the power God gives us to unfailingly preserve Christian convictions and the goal which they hold out in the midst of the outward circumstances which overwhelm us. If "faith" shows itself here with spontaneous power, we meet a more reflective notion in James 1:6, viz., doubt (διακρίνεσθαι) opposed to πίστις and preventing the answer to prayer. This psychological conception is necessarily introduced under the influence of experience with prayer. Why was the prayer not answered? Why did the miracle, so much desired and sought for, not occur? Among the possible answers, this is probably the oldest—faith is penetrated by doubt; hence, it is a matter of overcoming doubt. Such is achieved through humble prayer and fasting (Mark 9:29), but also by inner sanctification in general, for doubt clings to sin, from which it draws its nourishment. This then explains the connection between Mark 11:24 and 25: Whoever is not reconciled with God and has not received pardon for his sins cannot have the faith which moves mountains. An analogous idea is found in the Shepherd of Hermas, Mand. IX.[24]

We could penetrate further into the study of the connections between primitive Christian faith and the power which overcomes obstacles, but our study has another goal. In the following pages we will show that miracle was not only a source of power and joy for the first Christians, but that it also caused serious difficulties outside and even within the churches.

II.

Criticism Hostile to Jesus' Miracles

Miracle had deep roots in primitive Christianity. We simply cannot depict this era of our religion without miracles. But as we have already noted, Christian thaumaturgy also gave rise to all sorts of difficulties for the church. And as we can clearly see, these difficulties were not negligible.

There were, on the one hand, malevolent persons who declared, perhaps during his lifetime, that Jesus' *dynameis* were due to magic, and made him out a magician, an ally of Satan. On the other hand, embarrassments resulting from the excessive advance of thaumaturgy in the churches began to be noticed. It was necessary to fight against the menace of a religion become superficial, mechanical, indeed, even immoral. It even happened that some unscrupulous persons selfishly took advantage of the power to perform miracles and exploited the good faith of the brethren.

We will first examine Jesus' enemies' criticisms of his miracles and the apology which the church opposed to them. Then we will investigate the data which show that the miracles posed a problem for the very integrity of the church.

Jesus was originally accused of magic by the Jews who fought with any means against the sect of the crucified Messiah. We will have no trouble understanding how distressing this accusation was for the faithful. It appears to us that it was done to discredit the cause of Christianity. In this period, magic overran Palestine and surrounding countries, but was all the more contemptible in the eyes of every upright man. Hence, when Jesus was accused of being a magician, it could only deeply offend the religious sentiment of the Christians. For them, Jesus was just that great adversary and conqueror of demons, and consequently the enemy of all occult sciences. He could not be more monstrously slandered than to be accused of having himself exercised the diabolical craft of the magician.

In addition, the response was not at all easy to give. It could not be denied that a number of Jesus' miracles undoubtedly resembled magicians' sorceries. How could defense be conducted under such circumstances?

Very early, pagan polemicists seized the weapon originally forged by the Jews to discredit Christianity in the eyes of their cultured contemporaries. Whoever reads Origen against Celsus continually encounters the attempt at an apologetic and refutation provoked by the charge that Jesus used magic. Because it is worthwhile, we will give a general sketch of the ancient church's apologetic; then attempt to discover the first traces of the problem.

The variety of arguments shows how difficult this task was and, at the same time, allows us to glean from it the earliest apologetic tendencies.

Among critical voices raised on the subject of Jesus' *dynameis,* we will listen first to a most unusual one, less fanatic and malevolent than the others, but not without a certain acrimony. It is a criticism which allows us to puzzle out Jesus' response to the message of the captive Baptist in Matt. 11. Then we will fix our attention on the accusation that Jesus was an ally of Beelzebul (Mark 3), and on his defense against this calumny. Finally, we will examine a feature of the synoptic tradition which is very characteristic from our point of view —Jesus' enjoining the persons healed not to make him known.

THE MIRACLES OF JESUS IN THE ANCIENT CHURCH: CRITICISM AND APOLOGY

The testimonies of the oldest Christian authors show that it was precisely the Jews who accused Jesus of magic. *Justin,* in Dial. 69:5 expressly states:

> But though they saw such works, they asserted it was magical art (φαντασία μαγική). For they dared to call Him a magician, and a deceiver of the people. *(The Ante-Nicene Fathers,* I, 233).

Among other defamations, the Jew in *Celsus* relates that Jesus, of necessity having placed himself in the service of an Egyptian, had learned in Egypt some of the magical tricks which had made the Egyptians famous. Proud of these devices, he had returned to his own country, and by virtue of his powers publicly declared that he was God (Origen against Celsus I, 28). *Arnobius,* in Adv. Nat. I, 43 writes:

> My opponent will perhaps meet me .with many other slanderous and childish charges which are commonly urged. Jesus was a Magician; He effected all these things by secret art. From the shrines of the Egyptians He stole the names of angels of might, and the religious system of a remote country. *(The Ante-Nicene Fathers,* VI, 425).

The *Acta Sanctorum,* Febr. 1, 45b (authored by Pionius who died in A.D. 250) reads:

> The Jews say, moreover, that Christ had practised necromancy and that after the crucifixion he had raised himself by his own power.

And *Lactantius* writes in the Divin. Inst. IV, 15, 1:

> Those wonderful works, on account of which, though they were signs of heavenly power, the Jews esteemed Him (Christ) a magician (cf. also 13, 17). *(The Ante-Nicene Fathers,* VII, 114f.).

Jewish literature after the beginnings of Christianity identifies Jesus with the ill-famed *Ben Stada* who imported magic art from Egypt. Elsewhere it is told that Jesus had practiced magic and had seduced and misled Israel. It was even claimed that Jesus had been hanged the night of Passover for practicing magic. (All these passages are collected and interpreted in Strack-Billerbeck, *Kommentar zum Neuen Testament aus Talmud und Midrash* I, Munich, 1922, pp. 38ff.; 84ff.; 631ff.; cf. H. Strack, *Jesus, die Haeretiker und die Christen nach den ältesten jüdischen Angaben, Schriften des Institu-*

tum Judaicum in Berlin, Nr. 37, Leipzig, 1910; B. Pick, *Jesus in the Talmud,* Chicago, 1913).

This kind of approach perfectly suited the pagan polemic which asserted that not only Jesus, but also Moses, the prophets, the apostles and other Christian wonder-workers were charlatans, mountebanks, and professional exorcists. This is chiefly expressed in *Celsus. Porphyry* claims that the apostles performed their miracles by means of magical devices, as did the Egyptian magicians Apuleius and Apollonius of Tyana. Augustine also takes account of these calumnies.[25]

What follows is in essence the response of Christian apologetic (cf. W. Bauer, *Das Leben Jesu im Zeitalter der Neutestamentlichen Apokryphen,* pp. 366ff.) :

1. The miracles of Jesus were not due to chance or magic, but were predicted by the prophets in the Old Testament (cf. Justin, Apol. I, 30; Lactantius, Divin. Inst. V, 3, 18ff.; Tertullian, Adv. Marc. III, 3).

2. The church naturally felt the need to take up the question of the reality of these phenomena and in doing so used various approaches. One of the oldest arguments of apologetic called attention to the efficacy and *lasting effect* of Jesus' healings. According to *Eusebius,* Eccl. His. IV, 3, 2, Quadratus, in his apology to the emperor Hadrian declared that persons healed or resuscitated by Jesus had lived long after his departure, some of them even till these last times (ϵἰς τοὺς ἡμετέρους χρόνους), which proves Jesus' miracles were true ($\check{\epsilon}$ργα ἀληθῆ). According to an account of Philip of Side, *Papias* re-

lated an analogous situation (cf. E. Preuschen, *Antilegomena*, 2nd ed., 1905, p. 94). Against the Gnostics who said Jesus only pretended to do miracles, *Irenaeus* (II, 32, 4) affirms that the reality of Jesus' miracles is proven by the manner in which miracles are done in his name in the church— Christian exorcists "certainly and truly" drive out spirits, "even the dead are raised up, and have lived among us for many years" (cf. 31,2). The *Acta Petri* (Actus Vercellenses) 31 give us a lively illustration of the application of this criterion:

> But after a few days had elapsed Simon the magician promised the rabble that he would show Peter that he had not put his faith in the true God but in a deception. Now while he performed many false miracles, he was laughed to scorn by those disciples who were already firm (in the faith). For in their living-rooms he caused certain spirits to be brought to them, which were only appearances without real existence. And what more is there to say? Although he had often been convicted for his magic art, he made the lame appear to be sound for a short time, and the blind likewise, and once he appeared to make many who were dead come alive and move, as he did with Nicostratus. But all the while Peter followed him and exposed him to the onlookers (cf. E. Hennecke, *New Testament Apocrypha*, Vol. II, Philadelphia, 1965, p. 314f.).

3. The fact was then underlined that in performing his miracles Jesus did not use any kind of *device*. *Arnobius* especially insists on this point in Adv. Nat. I, 43, 44, 48:

> Without any power of incantations, without the juice of herbs and of grasses, without any anxious watching of sacrifices, of libations, or of seasons. *(The Ante-Nicene Fathers*, VI, 425).

Then in Chapter 50:

> In order that no lurking suspicion might remain
> of His having lavished these gifts and bounties by
> magic arts, from the immense multitude of people,
> which with admiring wonder strove to gain His
> favor, He chose fishermen, artisans, rustics, and
> unskilled persons of a similar kind, that they being
> sent through various nations should perform all
> those miracles without any deceit and without any
> material aids. *(The Ante-Nicene Fathers,* VI, 427).

Lactantius, Divin. Inst. IV, 15, 9, after having
enumerated Jesus' miracles, writes:

> And He performed all these things not by His
> hands, or the application of any remedy, but by
> His word and command (cf. Clem. Hom. I, 6:
> κελεύσει μόνῃ). *(The Ante-Nicene Fathers,* VII, 115).

Eusebius, Eccl. Hist. I, 13, 18, tells of the healing of
Abgar by Thomas and the astonishment of the king
over the apostle's healing him ἄνευ φαρμακείας καὶ
βοτανῶν.[26]

4. Finally, it was an interesting task to show that
Jesus as thaumaturge was sharply distinguished
from magicians and conjurers, because he acted
with a perfect *disinterestedness,* aiming only at
men's salvation. He sought neither ostentation nor
profit, and never used his power for evil ends.
Arnobius, Adv. Nat. I, 43ff., first describes the
magicians' tricks: They bring about a fatal epi-
demic; open what is closed without a key; they
strike people dumb and arouse among themselves
illicit love and fierce covetousness, etc. . . . but,

> if they seem to attempt anything useful, [they are]
> able to do it not by their own power, but by the
> might of those deities whom they invoke. *(The
> Ante-Nicene Fathers,* VI, 425).

Christ, however, accomplished all he did by the sheer power of his name. And that is not all, for

> as was the proper duty of *the* true God, as was con-
> sistent with His nature, as was worthy of Him, in
> the generosity of His bounteous power He bestowed
> nothing hurtful or injurious, but *only that which*
> is helpful, beneficial, and full of blessings good for
> men (I, 44; *The Ante-Nicene Fathers*, VI, 425).

Clem. Hom. II, 34, contrasts Jesus as thaumaturge with Simon Magus, the magician *par excellence*.[27] The σημεῖα attributed to Simon are ἀνωφελῆ, e.g., making statues walk, changing himself into a serpent or goat, flying through the air, etc. All these things are useless to men and serve only to trick them:

> But the miracles of compassionate truth are philan-
> thropic, such as you have heard the Lord did, and
> that I after him accomplish by my prayers. *(The
> Ante-Nicene Fathers, VIII, 235).*

Irenaeus uses the same argument against the Carpocratians in II, 31, 2ff. (cf. 32, 3) :

> Since, therefore, there exist among them error and
> misleading influences, and magical illusions are
> impiously wrought in the sight of men; but in the
> Church, sympathy, and compassion, and stedfast-
> ness, and truth, for the aid and encouragement of
> mankind, are not only displayed without fee or
> reward, but we ourselves lay out for the benefit of
> others our own means; and inasmuch as those who
> are cured very frequently do not possess the things
> which they require, they receive them from us (II,
> 31, 3; The *Ante-Nicene Fathers*, I, 407).

These are the main arguments which the Christians used against those who called Christ a magician and imposter, and who called them by the same names. But none of these arguments can be considered definitive. This explains the alternation and variety of viewpoints. The apologist's attitude betrays a certain embarrassment. As we already stated, no one examined this question more thoroughly than *Origen.* In his λόγος ἀληθής Celsus obviously spoke at length of the miracles narrated in the Gospels, and one of his best ploys was to present them as magician's tricks. A good dialectician, he skillfully pitted the horror which magic inspired in Christians against their own belief in miracles and the Christian practice of miracles, and Origen was forced to follow them in the mazes of his argumentation (I, 6, 28, 38, 46, 60, 68; II, 9, 14-16, 32, 35, 44, 48ff., 52, 56; IV, 27, 36; VIII, 9). It would be interesting to attempt to reconstruct Celsus' reasoning, but an endeavor of this kind would exceed the limits of this work. Naturally, Origen also makes use of the argument from Old Testament prophecy (I, 50, 53). He also underscores the fact that Jesus did not have recourse to the aid of demons, in imitation of the magicians, but quite the contrary, by his coming to earth he crippled the demons' power (I, 60). But the principal argument is the demonstration of Jesus' *moral personality:* Jesus did not perform his miracles to appear great, but to bring men to the knowledge of the truth and thus to create in them a superior moral and spiritual life: (cf. especially I, 38; II, 44). In I, 68 Origen writes:

> But, as it helped his purpose, he compared the (miracles) related of Jesus to the results produced by magic. There would indeed be a resemblance between them, if Jesus, like the dealers in magical

arts, had performed His works only for show; but now there is not a single juggler who, by means of his proceedings, invites his spectators to reform their manners, or trains those to the fear of God who are amazed at what they see, nor who tries to persuade them so to live as men who are to be justified by God. And jugglers do none of these things, because they have neither the power nor the will, nor any desire to busy themselves about the reformation of men, inasmuch as their own lives are full of the grossest and most notorious sins. But how should not He who, by the miracles which He did, induce those who beheld the excellent results to undertake the reformation of their characters, manifest Himself not only to His genuine disciples, but also to others, as a pattern of most virtuous life, in order that His disciples might devote themselves to the work of instructing men in the will of God, and that the others, after being more fully instructed by His word and character than by His miracles, as to how they were to direct their lives, might in all their conduct have a constant reference to the good pleasure of the universal God? And if such were the life of Jesus, how could any one with reason compare Him with the sect of imposters, and not, on the contrary, believe, according to the promise, that He was God, who appeared in human form to do good to our race? *(The Ante-Nicene Fathers, IV, 427)*.

These are the words of a theologian whose view espouses the tradition in the highest fashion and defends it with all the resources of a cultured intelligence, setting it within a vast unity of thought.

Let us retrace the course of history and take the viewpoint of a generation of Christians whose position in time did not allow a historical perspective, but who were fully immersed in the intense life of primitive Christianity. How was the problem of miracle posed for them? And how did they try to find its solution?

THE MESSAGE OF THE BAPTIST

After all we have just said, it is not surprising that little use was made of Jesus' miracles to demonstrate his divine mission. They were not exactly suited to this. Quite the contrary, from the beginning the greatest importance was attached to the Old Testament witness: Jesus, dead and risen, is the Savior foretold by the ancient prophets. This method is at times also applied to Jesus' miracles. Only against the background of the promises did the miracles acquire demonstrative force.

This idea is clearly set forth in *Justin* the apologist, Apol. I, 30. In beginning the demonstration of Christ's divinity, he writes:

> But lest any one should meet us with the question, What should prevent that He whom we call Christ, being a man born of men, performed what we call His mighty works by magical art (μαγικῇ τέχνῃ), and by this appeared to be the Son of God? we will now offer proof, not trusting mere assertions, but being of necessity persuaded by those who prophesied (of Him) before these things came to pass, for with our own eyes we behold things that have happened and are happening just as they were predicted; and this will, we think, appear even to you the strongest and truest evidence. *(The Ante-Nicene Fathers, I, 172f.)*

Tertullian expresses an analogous opinion in Adv. Marc. III, 3, by refusing, vis-a-vis Marcion, to legitimate Jesus' divine mission by his miracles *(per documenta virtutum)*. Tertullian refers to Jesus himself who predicted the miracles of false Messiahs. Only complete agreement with the prophets proves Jesus' divine sonship (cf. Irenaeus, Adv. Haer. II, 32, 4).

Lactantius speaks at length of miracles in Div. Inst. V, 3. His words are directed against the philosopher Hierocles who contrasts Apollonius of Tyana with Christ. Apollonius, he says, performed greater miracles than Christ, but did not claim to be God; his true disciples are really too well-informed to consider him as such. Jesus, by contrast, is only a pitiable charlatan, and his admirers madmen ("that it may be evident that we, who did not at once connect a belief in his divinity with wonderful deeds, are wiser than you, who on account of slight wonders believed that he was a god"). Lactantius adds this remark:

> It is not wonderful if you, who are far removed from the wisdom of God, understand nothing at all of those things which you have read, since the Jews, who from the beginning had frequently read the prophets, and to whom the mystery of God had been assigned, were nevertheless ignorant of what they read. Learn therefore, if you have any sense, that Christ was not believed by us to be God on this account, because He did wonderful things, but because we saw that all things were done in His case which were announced to us by the prediction of the prophets. He performed wonderful deeds: we might have supposed Him to be a magician, as you now suppose Him to be, and the Jews then supposed Him, if all the prophets did not with one accord proclaim that Christ would do those very

things. Therefore, we believe Him to be God, not more from His wonderful deeds and works, than from that very cross which you as dogs lick, since that also was predicted at the same time. It was not therefore on His own testimony (for who can be believed when he speaks concerning himself?), but on the testimony of the prophets who long before foretold all things which He did and suffered, that He gained a belief in His divinity, which could have happened neither to Apollonius, nor to Apuleius, nor to any of the magicians; nor can it happen at any time. *(The Ante-Nicene Fathers,* VII, 139).

Reflections of this sort give some clarity to a narrative of the synoptic tradition, whose meaning exegesis has not grasped with sufficient precision. It is the *response of Jesus to the Baptist* in Matt. 11:2-6. It is pointed out as a significant motif in the Baptist's question that in prison he had heard of Jesus' ἔργα. He then sent some of his disciples to Jesus to ask him this question, "Are you ὁ ἐρχόμενος, or shall we look for another?" Jesus answers by referring him precisely to his miracles, "go and tell John what you hear and see. . . ."

Indeed, not only the meaning of the Baptist's question, but also Jesus' response has been much discussed. How could Jesus' acts make such an impression on John? And how could Jesus' answer furnish the desired clarity? We need not examine the various explanations by which scholars have tried to resolve these difficulties. The problem is solved as soon as we ask what the importance of the Baptist's doubts and message were, as well as the importance of Jesus' answer to questions troubling the community of believers. Hardly another answer can be given, if not that the Baptist's question and Jesus' reply are calculated to eliminate the σκάνδαλον of the ἔργα of Jesus. Here especially we observe the lively criticism lodged against Jesus and his activity by the *followers of the Baptist*. Nearly all the evangelical tradition about John the Baptist is dominated by the intent to use him to enhance the person of Jesus. We sense the enormous tension which long existed between the disciples of John and those of Jesus. John himself announced Jesus, and as precursor, declared himself inferior to Jesus. Here was the most efficacious means available to Christian apologetic. In the present instance, John is intended to serve that apologetic. He poses as mouthpiece for the criticism of Jesus' miracles, all the while displaying the greatest respect by asking Jesus himself to instruct him and thus instigating authentic correction of the misunderstanding.

What then are the criticisms lodged by John's disciples against Jesus? He was undoubtedly reproached for limiting himself to healings and exorcisms, his action considered devoid of all messianic character. Jesus was only a cunning thaumaturge as many others of the same ilk, but with a bit more intelligence. This malicious criticism is transformed and takes on a straightforward quality in the mouth of the imprisoned Baptist, and nothing of his disciples' language remains except the significant word ὁ ἐρχόμενος (Matt. 3:11).

Jesus' reply retains its uniqueness by his use of the *prophetic formulas:*

The blind recover their sight, the lame walk,
lepers are cleansed, the deaf hear,
the dead arise, and the gospel is proclaimed
to the poor. . . . (cf. Isa. 29:18ff.; 35:5ff.; 61:1).

What is there to say except that these acts are not
those of a passing thaumaturge, but are the fulfillment of prophecies? From there it is only a step to
deciding the worth of their performer—he is precisely ὁ ἐρχόμενος. This then explains the final word:
"Blessed is he who takes no *offense* at me," that is
to say, blessed is the man who penetrates to this
relationship and without being superficial, is not at
all scandalized, does not take Jesus for a healer and
professional exorcist. The σκάνδαλον to be avoided is
the rather natural, but false estimation of Jesus'
miracles.[28]

Thus is settled the old debate concerning John's
message, whether due to sudden doubt, or to a pre-
sentiment first roused in him that Jesus might be
"he who was to come." In the mind of the evangelist, the Baptist's question quite probably represents a doubt to which Jesus gives the answer requested by quoting the prophets. Naturally, the
evangelist did not pose the question of how the
Baptist's doubt could be reconciled with his previous
experiences and earlier attitude to Jesus. His point
of departure is not that of psychology. What is
important is merely the apologetic value of the
doubt and its removal.

Here I am not in complete accord with what M.
Dibelius writes in his fine study, *Die urchristliche
Überlieferung von Johannes dem Täufer* (Göttin-
gen, 1911, pp. 33ff.). He underscores the fact, con-

stant in the Gospel tradition, that the Baptist serves
to glorify Jesus; whereas here he represents the
uncertainty confronting Jesus. Precisely this feature would guarantee the authenticity of the episode:

> Legend would not have allowed the Baptist, whom
> it portrayed as Jesus' herald, to give evidence of
> half-faith by his questions. Further, it would not
> have allowed the Savior, whom it had clothed in
> the Messiah's glory from the manger, to give such
> an indefinite answer (p. 37).

As we have seen, the Baptist's question by no
means changes his role as witness to the Messiah
Jesus—he merely gives an indirect witness. The
earlier exegetes were really not so poorly inspired
when they believed that by his message John the
Baptist did not intend so much to express his own
doubt as to bring his disciples to faith in Jesus
(Hilary, Ambrose, Chrysostom, Jerome and Cal-
vin). And Jesus' reply is not at all vague, if we
recall that the Baptist's question is directed to the
$\xi\rho\gamma\alpha$ of Jesus. Here we do not have the simple question, Are you the Messiah? but rather, Do these
acts have messianic character? (cf. $\xi\rho\gamma\alpha$ $\tau o\hat{\nu}$ $X\rho\iota\sigma\tau o\hat{\nu}$
in Matt. 11:2). The answer is decisive; they are the
promised blessings of the messianic era. Then we
are not permitted with Dibelius to dismiss the preliminary remark in Matt. 11:2 as if it had been
formulated by the evangelist, or to consider John's
question and Jesus' response in isolation. It is equal-
ly false to say with Zahn that $\tau\grave{\alpha}$ $\xi\rho\gamma\alpha$ denotes all
Jesus' activity (cf. Luke 7:18, and the meaning of
$\xi\rho\gamma\alpha$ in the fragment of Quadratus in Eusebius, Eccl.
Hist. IV, 3, 2).

This does not mean, of course, that the tradition of the captive Baptist's message to Jesus is without historical foundation; it is quite probable that messengers came and went from one to the other. But the content of this tradition, everything which gives it its concrete character, has a certain objective.

It is remarkable that the pericope of the Baptist's question is immediately followed by threats against those cities which did not repent because of Jesus' *dynameis* (11:20-24). After this comes the terrible accusation that Jesus made a pact with the devil, followed by Jesus' response (12:22f.). The question of the value of the miracles is thus posed on different occasions in the section containing Chapters 11 and 12. But if the attitude of John's disciples toward Jesus' miracles was critical, it was not directly hostile. The healings and the exorcisms were entirely legitimate acts; we have only to think of the miracles of the ancient prophets, Moses, Elijah, and Elisha. In his defense, Jesus puts this question, "And if I cast out demons by Beelzebul, by whom do your sons cast them out? Therefore they shall be your judges." Thus, thanks to a special gift, there were among the people some who healed the sick and cast out demons and enjoyed general esteem. Why then should Jesus be refused the same esteem? No doubt, John's disciples conceded this.[29] But Jesus intended to be Messiah, or rather, his disciples claimed this title for him. This attitude aroused critcism on the part of John's disciples, for the Messiah should be something more and something else.

The Nazarene's desperate and unyielding adversaries went still further. They went so far as to hurl the appalling accusation that Jesus was only a dangerous thaumaturge, that he practiced diabolical artifices, and that he was an imposter. We hear an echo of these calumnies and the defense against them in the passages in Mark 3:22ff.; Matt. 12:22ff. and Luke 11:14ff.

"IT IS ONLY BY BEELZEBUL THAT HE CASTS OUT DEMONS"

Mark relates in 3:20ff. that when Jesus arrived "home," the crowd gathered so that they (Jesus and his disciples) did not even have time to eat. It is not expressly stated that Jesus healed the sick, but it is obvious according to the general description which precedes in 3:9-12. Then the scribes, come down from Jerusalem, accuse Jesus of being allied with Beelzebul.

On the other hand, we learn that Jesus' kin set out to seize him, because, they said, he had lost his mind (ἐξέστη). This remark prepares for the narrative of the arrival of Jesus' mother and brothers who wished to summon him back (3:31ff.), and which in turn elicited Jesus' word about his true kin. There is little doubt that if Mark makes Jesus' family declare he has lost his mind, it is due to the accusation that he had made a pact with the devil. Jesus' conduct was suspect and could give rise to the worst interpretations. Naturally, Jesus' mother and brothers, themselves skeptical of the healings and exorcisms, give the most indulgent explanation which quite resembles an excuse—he has lost his mental equilibrium, he is not responsible. This is a psychological feature which we must assign to Mark. Mark probably felt that Jesus, in the words of vs. 35, made a thrust at a lack of understanding —"whoever does the *will of God* is my brother," that is, Jesus, when he heals and casts out demons, is doing the will of God; he is fulfilling his divine mission, and whoever imitates him is for him.

But the scribes from Jerusalem were saying, "he is possessed by Beelzebul, and by the prince of demons he casts out the demons." Jesus' answer is divided into two parts: First, he shows in parables (παραβολή, 3:23) the meaninglessness of this accusation (vss. 23b-26); then he makes it clear that he had to be victor over the devil so as to cast out the demons (vs. 27). He concludes by threatening the slanderers whose accusation has made them guilty of an unpardonable sin (cf. the explanation of this word which I proposed in the *Revue d'Histoire et de Philosophie religieuses*, 1923, pp. 367ff.).

We must analyze the accusation and the defense in greater detail.

The text of the accusation is that Jesus is possessed by Beelzebul (Βεελζεβοὺλ ἔχει, cf. δαιμόνιον ἔχει in Matt. 11:18), and thus makes use of the mightiest demon (ὁ ἄρχων τῶν δαιμονίων) against the weaker. Matthew and Luke, in reproducing this episode, evidently draw from the collection of Jesus' speeches and identify Beelzebul with the prince of demons. If the tenor of Mark's text allows another interpretation, there is still no basic difference. In any case, Jesus is accused of casting out demons with the aid of a particularly powerful evil spirit. At first sight, this idea is quite remarkable; the contradiction it contains is obvious, and the defense quite fair. In my epilog to the study of S. Eitrem, *Die Versuchung Christi* (Oslo, 1924), I maintained the point of view (p. 33) that the accusation originally and in general fashion considered Jesus' miracles as the workings of a magician. Apologetic has slightly altered this charge so as to refute it more easily and impressively—among the miracles of Jesus there were also exorcisms. Jesus thus used diabolical tricks to cast out the devil. Impossible! In this form the accusation would then have been adapted to the needs of the defense.

This solution, however, is not without disadvantage since the accusation takes a very characteristic form. We must especially consider the term Beelzebul, a concrete feature whose origin certainly goes back to the slanders against Christ. It is true that in his final remark (vs. 30), Mark does not attach importance to the distinction between Beelzebul and the other demons, and declares in a very general manner ὅτι ἔλεγον, πνεῦμα ἀκάθαρτον ἔχει. Nevertheless, in making this statement he has only the general notion of blasphemy in mind (vss. 28ff.). Hence we can only suppose that Jesus' adversaries accused him of having worked his miracles for selfish reasons, merely for setting himself up before men as a great exorcist. For this purpose it was very useful for him to be allied with the ἄρχων τῶν δαιμονίων, with whose aid he could conquer the less powerful demons.

We have here an altogether popular notion. The thaumaturge holds in his power the demon inhabiting him, and the higher the demon's rank, the greater the power of the thaumaturge. In this way he can exorcise and conquer the lesser spirits. Hence the thaumaturge's great concern is to achieve communication with the mightiest spirits. This idea stems from a very old and popular *pluralism* according to which the spirits are legion in number and quite varied in quality and capacity. Even if all are, so to speak, of the same family, comprising a whole including many groups and classes, the ties uniting them are tenuous and it is not out of the question that one might supplant or attack the other.

It is interesting, then, to observe how the defense in Mark 9:23ff. opposes to this naive pluralism a rigorously *monistic* view of the spirit-world. How can Satan cast out Satan? In some way, this brings to mind 1 Cor. 12, where Paul develops the thesis that "there are varieties of gifts, but the same Spirit." In both cases a monistic view is opposed to popular pluralism.

Jesus' defense in Mark 3 requires a more precise explanation. In reality, it consists of several apologetic motifs which have been joined together. Mark records two parables and one threat; the collection of dominical sayings (Q) has inserted between the two parables a completely incongruous argument (Matt. 12:27ff.; Luke 11:19ff.), and the threat is not found there at all.

In sum, the argument of Mark 3:23ff. is only the contrivance of a dialectician—the adversary is caught in a contradiction which really does not lie in his thought, but in the sheer logic of the image. It is quite possible that when Jesus was once re-

proached for exorcising demons by Beelzebul, he
confidently answered with a smile: Devil against
devil? some strategy! These words, in Jesus' mouth,
are most certainly *ironic;* one would particularly
like to assign him the concise formula in Mark, but
not in Q: πῶς δύναται Σατανᾶς Σατανᾶν ἐκβάλλειν. But whatever the origin of this speech, the evangelists sense
no irony in it. On the contrary, they sense the grav-
est seriousness. Against the popular notion they
appeal to Christian demonology to defend the master against an abominable calumny. For the Christian, evil spirits form a realm tightly organized
under Satan's direction (cf. ἡ βασιλεία αὐτοῦ in Matt.
12:26 and Luke 11:18). Thus the inherent logic of
the image of the divided kingdom not only consti-
tutes the point of the parable, but also has an actual
basis.

The fragment inserted in Matt. 12:27ff. and Luke
11:19ff. introduces an apologetic method quite different from the one we have just followed. It is a
dialectic based on images. All at once we have here
an *argumentum ad hominem:*

> And if I cast out demons by Beelzebul,
> By whom do your sons cast them out?

The meaning of these words is clear. The same
accusation of an alliance with the devil would strike
Jewish exorcists as well. In fact, an effective
counter-attack was originally concentrated in this
brief question. But this quick reply has been amplified and enlarged by tradition—"therefore they
shall be your judges. . . ."

These words are evidently part of a secondary

formation and are the faint echo of a caustic retort. The same holds true for the other speech which is linked to the preceding:

> But if it is by the Spirit of God that I cast out demons, then the kingdom of God has come upon you.

The interruption in the sequence of ideas is very interesting. From the formal point of view, this speech is linked to the preceding in such fashion that each of the two conditional clauses introduces one of the alternative terms.

> If I cast out demons by Beelzebul. . . .
> If I cast out demons by the Spirit of God. . . .

But the clauses subsequent to these correlative clauses are totally incongruous. The Jewish exorcists in the first of these clauses have suddenly disappeared in the second, for it cannot be concluded their exorcisms were also signs of the coming of the kingdom of God. The disparity of the two correlative clauses proves that the second was added later. Apologetic was not after settling for the pure and simple retort. For its completion it needed the reverse of the calumny. Given the form of the conclusion ($\epsilon i \ \dot{\epsilon} \gamma \dot{\omega}$ . . .), two disparate thoughts were combined into a single scheme.

In Mark, a *second parable* (3:27) is immediately joined to the first, so that to all appearances we have two parables (as in Mark 4:30ff.; Matt. 13:31-33; 44-46; Luke 14:28-32; 15). But let us not be deceived! The combination is not original as we saw in Q. The second similitude is not a true parable, but rather an allegorical refutation of the adver-

saries' slanders. That Jesus casts out demons implies
he has conquered their supreme leader. Here, the
concrete idea assumes the form of a *general* proposition: "Or how can one enter a strong man's
house . . . ?" Christian apologetic learned early to
make use of a form which gave its affirmations the
persuasive force proper to the logic of the parables.
A. Jülicher *(Die Gleichnisreden Jesu,* 2nd ed., 1910,
II, p. 226) formulates the particular meaning of the
first similitude: "It is not Satan who casts out
here. . . ." In the second parable which is allegorical
in character he finds this idea: "Satan himself is
struck by the exorcisms." For my part, I am of the
opinion that from Mark's point of view we must
take the terms "to bind" and "the strong man" in
their technical sense, even if these notions appear
in the totality of a similitude using general terms.
Though Q (Luke) offers us an image with more
detail, the interpretation stands out all the more,
for it speaks expressly of the victory of *the* "strong-
est" over the "strong man" (ὁ ἰσχυρότερος can hardly
denote "*a* stronger man," as in Luke 3:16).

The monism of Christian demonology is also im-
plied and indirectly underscored in this speech.
From Jesus' victories over the demons we must
conclude that he had previously bound the prince of
spirits. This is the only interpretation which would
conform not only to the situation, but also to the
logic of all analogous experience. We read again in
Q (Luke 11:23):

> He who is not with me is against me,
> and he who does not gather with me scatters.

Taken in the sense of Q, this word can only express the rigorous unity and absolute solidarity of the world of spirits. It appears we have a proverb here (cf. W. Nestle and A. Fridrichsen in *Zeitschrift für neutestl. Wissenschaft* XIII, 1912, pp. 84ff., 273ff., and *Theologische Rundschau* XX, 1917, pp. 326ff.), of such a type that we must not stress the ἐμοῦ overmuch, as if this pronoun must necessarily refer to Jesus himself. Rather, its meaning is this: If the maxim "either/or" is the rule in the kingdom of Satan, how then can there be talk of the one fighting the other?

This group of logia in Q ends with the speech about the exorcised *demon* who later *returns* (Luke 11:24-26). No doubt, we have here the trace of a thesis quoted in favor of Jesus' victories over the demons. He achieved lasting results, whereas other exorcists could give the possessed only temporary relief—soon the last state of these persons became worse than the first. As we have already shown, the apologetic of the ancient church occasionally underlined the effectiveness of Jesus' healings.

Primitive Christianity was aware of its superiority over Jewish exorcists. Christians knew they had a more effective means than any their adversaries could use, and that was the name of Jesus. Strong in this conviction, they at times allowed the Jewish exorcists to use this name (Mark 9:38ff.), though with the sharp competition in missionizing, the exorcist did not always know how to keep himself at such a high level (Acts 19:13-16). *Justin* (Dial. 85, 10) also recognizes the success of Jewish exorcists when they adjure the demons in the name of

the God of their fathers. But he adds that Jewish
exorcists often used the same techniques as the
pagans: incense and formulas to bind the demons
(καταδεσμοί). Christians abstained from such practices which they considered magical.

Healings done by similar means were considered
a *pretense at miracle,* and it was believed that the
demons took advantage of these opportunities to
make sport of and deceive men, and that these healings were without real value (cf. *Tatian* Or. Ad.
Graec. Chap. 18; *Minucius Felix,* Oct. XXVII, 5).
Irenaeus also takes this point of view when he
speaks of Gnostic thaumaturges: can they cast out
demons other than those they themselves evoked
(Adv. Haer. II, 31, 2)? Their miracles are only
sorcery and hoax, their effect soon wears off and
lasts only an instant (II, 32, 3), whereas the exorcists of the church "certainly and truly" cast out
demons (II, 32, 4).

JESUS' INJUNCTION TO SILENCE

The Gospel of Mark repeatedly relates that Jesus
commanded those whom he healed to tell no one of
their healing; further, that he enjoined the demons
he exorcised to silence when they called him the
"Holy One of God;" finally, that he strictly charged
his disciples not to make known that he was Messiah.

As we know, these characteristic features form
the basis of W. Wrede's theory of the "messianic
secret" *(Das Messiasgeheimnis,* Göttingen, 1901).
Wrede challenges the idea that Jesus wished to be
Messiah. Only after his death, under the influence

of the events of Easter, did this belief originate with his disciples. This belief led to an alteration of the historical recollections concerning Jesus and his activity; already during his life-time he allegedly showed himself as Messiah. In order to avoid the contradiction between the historical reality and the dogmatic conception, the messianic character of Jesus was portrayed as a secret which Jesus only gradually revealed to his disciples (but they were indifferent and did not understand). As for the people, Jesus tried to conceal his dignity from them by enjoining to silence the men and spirits who recognized him.

The great problem raised by Wrede in his celebrated work need not be discussed here. We will content ourselves with examining the tradition according to which Jesus, after having performed a miracle, forbade that it be reported. In general, we must oppose Wrede when he sets all Jesus' injunctions to silence under the same rubric so as to exploit them in favor of his theory. Such a method is unsound. We must carefully distinguish between three groups (the demons, those healed, and the disciples) and examine them separately. The problem is to see whether the prohibition is an original element of the tradition or a later addition adopted by Mark, or the work of the Gospel's redactor himself. Only by considering these questions can we discover why Jesus commanded silence.

1. *The Demons.* Only the pericope in Mark 1:23-28 concerns us here (since 1:34 and 3:12 belong to general descriptions which are the work of the evangelist). There it is said that when the unclean

spirit in the demoniac recognized Jesus it cried out, "What have you to do with us, Jesus of Nazareth? Have you come to destroy us? I know who you are, the Holy One of God." Jesus rebuked him severely and said, "Be silent, and come out of him!" Then the unclean spirit, convulsing him and crying with a loud voice, came out of him.

To the question whether this narrative was cast in one piece or has been amplified in its present form the answer is clear. The demon who cries aloud when exorcised forms a characteristic feature of these narratives (cf. 9:26). He knows his conqueror and calls him by name—again a well-known feature in narratives which tell of the healing of demoniacs (Mark 5:7: Ἰησοῦ υἱὲ τοῦ θεοῦ τοῦ ὑψίστου, cf. Acts 16:17). The order to the demons to keep silent is also part of the exorcism scheme. Πεφίμωσο is really a formula of exorcism, as Mark 4:39 shows: Jesus says to the wind and waves σιώπα, πεφίμωσο (φιμοῦν means καταδεῖν, cf. E. Rohde, *Psyche*, New York 1925, p. 604, and M. Dibelius, *Die urchristliche Überlieferung von Johannes dem Täufer*, p. 37n.). Thus only when the demon keeps silent is his power completely broken and he is completely subject to the will of the exorcist.

If we examine the pericope in Mark 1:23-28 from this point of view, we see immediately that one of its components is an addition—the name of the exorcist. Here we have a veritable confession of faith —"we know who you are. . . ." But why this long and prolix discourse at the very moment of greatest danger? Only one answer can be given—here again we note the requirements of an apologetic of which we are amply aware. The demon himself defends Jesus against the slander of being a magician. Before everyone he confesses Jesus as the Holy One of God. This revelation suits the intent of the first redactor of the narrative so well that he even provoked it. Still, the πεφίμωσο remains where it is, for the word is part of the technique of exorcism.

But this was not Mark's intention. He explains the prohibition to speak by analogy with that given to the disciples about Jesus' messiahship (8:30). He adheres to the viewpoint contained in the summary accounts which he gives of Jesus' activity in 1:32ff. and 3:11ff. In the first of these passages we read "and (he) cast out many demons; and he would not permit the demons to speak, because they knew him." In the second passage, "and whenever the unclean spirits beheld him, they fell down before him and cried out, 'You are the Son of God.' And he strictly ordered them not to make him known."

Originally, the purpose of this injunction was not to conceal anything, but to paralyze the unclean spirit. Mark's special application of it is certainly second hand. But by noting this fact we have shed light on a new feature of the oldest apology for miracle—Jesus' rehabilitation by the demons themselves. After the words of the spirit in 1:24, it can no longer be doubted by what power Jesus casts out demons. How can one speak of an alliance with and help from Beelzebul when the spirits themselves call Jesus the Holy One of God?

2. *The Healings.* Here we need to examine the fol-

lowing pericopes: Mark 1:40-45 (the leper); 5:21-43 (Jairus' daughter); 7:31-37 (the deaf-mute), and 8:22-26 (the blind man from Bethsaida).

What all these stories have in common is that Jesus prevents either the one healed or his circle of friends from speaking to others of the cure. Mark 1:43ff.: "And he sternly charged him, and sent him away at once, and said to him, 'See that you say nothing to any one.'" Mark 5:43: "And he strictly charged them that no one should know this." Mark 7:36: "And he charged them to tell no one." The passage in 8:26 gives us a confused text; but it appears that Jesus wants to keep the news of the healing from spreading throughout the city.

There are also two instances where the person healed tells of his healing despite the prohibition:

> But he went out and began to talk freely about it, and to spread the news, so that Jesus could no longer openly enter a town, but was out in the country; and people came to him from every quar- (Mark 7:36).

> And he charged them to tell no one; but the more he charged them, the more zealously they proclaimed it. . . . "He has done all things well; he even makes the deaf hear and the dumb speak" (Mark 7:36).

We may confidently assert the purely literary and secondary character of narratives which relate the disobedience of those who were healed. In the first seven chapters which describe Jesus' activity among the people, we observe—and this is typical of the style of this kind of narrative—that the miracle

story ends with a very conventional reference to
the amazement, admiration, or fear of the crowd at
the sight of what took place; to conversations people had among themselves concerning it, and to the
fact that they went to Jesus en masse. This peculiar feature is rarely lacking in Chapters 1-7, save
for exceptional cases (the healing of Peter's mother-
in-law in 1:30ff. is really a family episode; the
Syro-Phoenician woman encounters Jesus in Gentile
territory in 7:24-30; the healing of the man with
the withered hand in 3:1-6 belongs to the series of
conflicts relating to the Sabbath; in the house of
Jairus the ἔκστασις is already anticipated by the small
circle grouped around the sick bed). When it is said
in the sections we have just examined that the person healed spread the news of his cure despite the
prohibition, it is to connect the miracle (which
occurred separately and about which Jesus commanded silence) to the conventional framework
formed by the description of the crowd's state of
mind.

But what about the injunction? Is it an integral
part of the primitive tradition? We cannot give an
exact judgment of 8:26 because it is evident the
text of this passage is altered. On the other hand,
5:43 and 7:36 altogether give the impression of
being literary accounts. We detect the hand of the
evangelist in the monotony of expression (cf. especially διαστέλλεσθαι in Mark 5:43; 7:36; 8:15; 9:9).
Further, the situation in the house of the synagogue
leader does not absolutely agree with the express
charge to tell no one. As for Matthew and Luke,
they arrange the Markan injunctions to silence in

their own way. It is particularly interesting to see how Matthew has been able to use these elements from a purely aesthetic point of view, as in 9:30, so as to round off the brief narrative of a healing (of the two blind men).

The passage in Mark 1:43ff. still remains. Jesus charges the man he has healed to do what the law prescribes; to be sure, this is not Mark's idea. It is rather a feature he found in the tradition. Jesus' attitude toward the law does not interest him. But it does interest the tradition, for it is a matter of emphasizing the loyalty of Jesus the thaumaturge to Moses. Hence it is quite probable that the injunction in this section is older than Mark's redaction, and that it has an apologetic tendency as well. In the pericope 12:15-20, Matthew gives an apt explanation of this tendency:

> And many followed him, and he healed them all, and ordered them not to make him known. This was to fulfill what was spoken by the prophet Isaiah: "Behold, my servant whom I have chosen, my beloved with whom my soul is well pleased, I will put my Spirit upon him, and he shall proclaim justice to the Gentiles. *He will not wrangle or cry aloud, nor will anyone hear his voice in the streets.*"

Thus Jesus was not a charlatan who used any means to publicize himself, as did ordinary thaumaturges. On the contrary, he expressly forbade those whom he healed to make their healing known.

Needless to say, this feature could after all be historical. Exactly what considerations prompted Jesus we can only guess. Perhaps it was aversion to all publicity; perhaps also concern for the soul of the one he healed. Later, however, this factor was taken up and brought to light in the struggle with slanders against Jesus. When he was portrayed as a sorcerer of great note, the Christian response was that all publicity was alien to him. Rather than clinging to those whom he healed, making them march before his triumphal car, using them to spread his fame, he sent them away and strictly charged them to keep silent—the opposite extreme of the practices of ordinary healers. In *Lucian* we see how they went about it. He describes Alexander of Abonoteichus and Peregrinus Proteus as incomparable masters of publicity.

It is true that in Mark 5:19 we are told that Jesus commanded the man he healed to tell others of his healing:

> Go home to your friends, and tell them how much the Lord has done for you, and how he has had mercy on you.

But here we are in Gentile territory; the story is of the Gerasene demoniac whom Jesus rescued from a vast number of demons. Jesus' words following the healing are the voice of the *missionary* who uses the miracle to propagate the faith. In primitive Christianity as in all other missionary work, propaganda was carried on in large part by the *family*. When anyone had experienced the blessings of the new religion, this event had great influence among his relatives and those who lived in the same house.

Jesus' repeated command to his *disciples* not to make him known is a special problem which we will omit from our account for the time being (cf. p. 70, *supra*).

Now we have come to see that miracle in primitive Christianity was not merely the object of special apologetic in response to the attacks of unbelievers, but that it was also regarded as a problem in the very midst of the church.

III.

The Problem of Miracle
in the Church

As already stated, a certain reaction soon emerges in the church against the naive elation inspired by the miracles and against the excesses of Christian thaumaturgy. This occurred partly for interior reasons, i.e. reasons of a religious nature, and partly because the *dynameis* were being abused. We can detect one such religious critique of thaumaturgy at the base of *the story of Jesus' temptation* as told by Matthew and Luke. In the pericope of the *healing of the paralytic* (Mark 2) we find another indication of the same reaction. A further separate feature of the religious critique of miracle is found preserved in one of the oldest strata of the tradition —Jesus' speech in Luke 10:17-20, which we will examine particularly from this point of view. Then we will call to mind Paul's polemic in 1 Cor. 13, which will also serve to clarify this question. Interference was made on behalf of the inner life of Christianity and its spiritual character, and attention was drawn to the fact that it was in peril of becoming an outward practice and a mechanical operation. This was soon a real danger. In the country of the gospel's origin, in the Hellenistic world, a good many believers of Jewish descent, excited by experience with divine powers at their disposal, were in danger of being absorbed in the miraculous, and of neglecting the foundation of the new life, viz., the salvation of the soul. It was not long after that Paul saw his young congregation at Corinth threatened with foundering on unbridled enthusiasm and felt constrained to lay greatest stress on love, that sober and practical virtue.

Viewed from this angle, the *Gospel of John* will pose an interesting but difficult problem. The Johannine discourses not only furnish a parenesis which is fixed in its main features and in its decisive expression which instills the indispensable moral duty of a truly Christian life, but the same Gospel also renders a judgment on miracle. This judgment is two-sided, indicating an intrinsic difficulty in the problem. The motifs and premises of this contradictory attitude toward miracle need not be examined here (cf. K. L. Schmidt, *Der johanneische Charakter der Erzählung vom Hochzeitswunder in Kana* in "Harnack-Ehrung," Leipzig, 1921, pp. 32ff.). We will reserve this question for a study soon to appear which will deal with the various Johannine problems.

What we must treat here is the New Testament polemic against *false prophets* and their abuses of miraculous forces. We must pay particular attention to this very serious problem in the primitive church.

THE TEMPTATION NARRATIVE

The narrative of Jesus' temptation by the devil in Matt. 4:1-11 and Luke 4:1-12 (cf. Mark 1:12-13) has always caused exegesis great difficulties. The problem which especially interested the earlier theologians was that of knowing how Jesus was able to be tempted and led by the devil (cf. P. Ketter, *Die Versuchung Jesu*, Münster i. W., 1918, pp. 87ff.). What also struck them was Satan's visibility and the rapid movement from one place to another. In our time, scholars have not always known how to understand this story. Here Jesus is the center of an episode of the mythical, or rather, legendary type, whereas elsewhere he moves in a sphere which completely conforms to reality. Though at times he moves about in a supernatural way, the topographical framework is nonetheless concrete and clear. But here there is first the desert, then, all of a sudden, the pinnacle of the temple at Jerusalem, and finally, a very high mountain, from which the whole earth could be seen at a glance.

The ancients who felt the same difficulty thought of a dream or vision. Modern exegetes choose to see in this story a parable or allegory, in which form Jesus gave his intimate experiences, or again, merely a Christian invention for the purpose of defending the thesis that Jesus was without sin. It is also supposed that it originated in reflections upon motifs drawn from the Old Testament (H. J. Holtzmann and others). But the most widespread opinion is that this story represents an *apologetic* tendency which should demonstrate that if Jesus did not fit the idea of the Messiah commonly held by the Jews, it was because this idea came from the devil (e.g., Joh. Weiss). We wish to examine this latter interpretation a bit more closely.

The story of the temptation is supposed to dispel a false messianic ideal. Jesus was not to establish his rule by the facile means of miracle, or by submitting himself to the prince of this world, but by his suffering and death. However interesting this interpretation may be, it certainly does not convey the historical sense of the narrative. At most it is an ingenious homiletic interpretation of the pericope. First of all, the two miracles (changing stones to bread and flying through the air) are not specifically messianic in character. The idea that by doing the devil homage Jesus would establish the messianic reign is truly absurd. Then, a point which never ceases to be an embarrassment to this type exegesis is that according to the entire tradition, Jesus was a well-known thaumaturge: He transformed water into wine; walked on water, fed thousands with a few loaves of bread, etc. According to the primitive church, it is precisely by great wonders that his character and divine power are manifested. How can all this be reconciled with the interpretation just noted?

In his remarkable book *Der Sohn Gottes* (Göttingen, 1916, pp. 139ff.; cf. 64ff.), Gillis A. P. Wetter has very ably shown that the temptation story reflects the general Christian conception according to which the Son of God as such performs miracles and only the most extraordinary. Wetter's thesis is that the "Son of God" idea has the same content in the Gospels as in Hellenism. From this he concludes that the title given to Jesus, υἱὸς τοῦ θεοῦ, is not of Jewish but Hellenistic origin. An essential feature of the "Son of God" in Hellenism is precisely his ability to work miracles. This explained, Wetter goes on to discuss the temptation story, giving particular emphasis to the twice-repeated εἰ υἱὸς εἰ τοῦ θεοῦ. It is clear that in this instance the miracles serve to prove Jesus' divine sonship. Wetter again remarks that we cannot uncover any connection between these miracles and Jewish messianic hopes; the miracles belong rather to the Hellenistic type savior who has a more general character. In the last temptation, however, he believes he recognizes the ideas of Jewish messianism.

Here we cannot discuss the question whether the "Son of God" idea in the synoptics is originally Jewish or Hellenistic. As presented, it includes the ideas of miraculous power and acts of such power. But if the miracles are inherent in the nature of the Son of God, and if Jesus is accurately portrayed in the Gospels as a thaumaturge, why then are the miracles so forcibly spurned as a temptation of the devil? Wetter does not answer this question.

At this point, S. Eitrem, in his suggestive study on *Die Versuchung Christi* has brought an interesting point of view to the discussion. Here, to his mind, is what the temptation involved: The devil wants to lure Jesus into practicing *magic*, but the narrative intends to defend Jesus against the reproach of magic. Transforming stones into bread and flying through the air are typical magical feats. Owning the riches and pleasures of the world is

precisely the goal the magician wishes to reach.
Eitrem has let himself be guided by a sound intui-
tion, and in order to shed light on each idea, he has
assembled much valuable material. But when it
comes to details, his thesis must be modified by giving more careful consideration to the facts and the
texts. Taking our point of departure from Wetter
and Eitrem, we shall now attempt to define the connection between the temptation narrative and the
problems discussed in the ancient church.

What exactly is the situation? Satan, we are told,
urges Jesus to do various miracles and gives as his
reason that Jesus is "Son of God." The εἰ υἱὸς εἶ τοῦ
θεοῦ ought in no way throw Jesus' divine sonship in
doubt, but rather concludes from an undoubted fact:
Since you are the Son of God, demonstrate this
divine power which is in you by these miracles! But
this is precisely what Jesus considers a *temptation*
and rejects it by quoting the words of Scripture.

This narrative must have originated in a Christian milieu where the need to see miracles, excessive
with the mass of believers, consequently provoked
criticism and apprehension. And this for religious
as much as for apologetic reasons. We have already
had opportunity to learn the apologetic viewpoint.
Here we will occupy ourselves with considerations
of a religious nature. Certain of the faithful in the
primitive church felt the need to set limits to pious
fantasy because they recognized that the wild
growth of the prodigious represented a danger
within and without. It was not only a matter of
curbing pious imagination which desired to make of
Jesus a thaumaturge after the cut of the magician,

but it was also necessary to protect the practice of piety against total degeneration and prevent Christianity from being reduced to a magical technique. The dispute between Jesus and the devil reflects arguments between the faithful and the representatives of a religion of miracle. The former went so far as to say that the crowd's ideas concerning the character and activity of the Son of God were only an invention of the devil. The evil one himself had proposed to Jesus an activity of this kind, but Jesus had emphatically spurned it.

Now we understand not only this specific formula-like phrase: εἰ υἱὸς εἶ τοῦ θεοῦ, but also the fact that it stems from the passionate defenders of the tradition and practice of miracles. Naturally, these Christians energetically affirm that Jesus, because and in so far as he was Son of God, could and was obliged to perform all manner of miracles. The notion υἱὸς τοῦ θεοῦ thus became the chief phrase in debates among Christians.

How may we more fully characterize those who criticized the popular notion? They take their arguments from Scripture with great skill. They are the *Christian scribes,* with a culture superior to that of the great majority. The others, of course, try equally to rely on words of Scripture so as to defend their particular view, but are completely outdone by the genuinely superior interpretation of their opponents. Credit is due Arnold Meyer (in *Festgabe Hugo Bluemner,* Zurich, 1914, pp. 143ff.), for having vigorously emphasized the theological character of the temptation story. The principle as strictly applied is that Scripture settles the question. Thus the specific situation created is that the devil quoted Scripture and was defeated by the words of Scripture.

We can glean an idea of the spiritual level of the two groups by carefully comparing their use of Scripture. One group chooses passages corresponding to its preference for the extraordinary and miraculous. The other has a more cultivated taste and a profounder religious sense; it prefers words which call for patience, humility and submission to God's will. We must not of course imagine that the latter group on principle rejected miracle; such is impossible. It does not deny that Jesus would have been able to transform stones into bread or would have been miraculously saved during a mortal fall; but what is more important than the bread of the body is the word of God for the soul, and one must keep from inciting miracle. This group undoubtedly distinguished miracles for men's salvation, which attended Jesus' activity, from other possible, though absurd and fanciful miracles, which can only corrupt healthy piety and discredit the faith in the eyes of Jews and Gentiles. Two miracles in this category are presented in the temptation story as temptations of the devil—to change stones to bread and to soar through the air. This is pure magic, such as was practiced by Simon Magus and other imposters (cf. Eitrem). Hence the first two temptations vie for a thaumaturgic view of the concept "Son of God." But it is a question whether we should consider this view as specifically Hellenistic (Wetter) or not rather as genuinely popular and Jewish as well as Hellenistic or Greek.

The third temptation remains. The devil leads Jesus to a very high mountain and shows him the kingdoms of the world and their splendor. "All these I will give you, if you will fall down and worship me." Here we have *an actual temptation*. In the first two cases, we easily recognize the work of a speculative and systematic mind. But the scene on the high mountain, with its marvelous view, is of extraordinary and impressive grandeur, though the redactor has drastically reduced the description in order to set this scene in the same dialog setting as the other temptations. Even superficially, i.e. seen merely from the formula of an identical introduction, these two temptations prove their relation over against the third. In other words, the third temptation originates in a primitive tradition, the same, perhaps, which is preserved to us piecemeal in the brief notice of Mark 1:12-13. The author of the temptation story, as it is transmitted to us, has incorporated it into his composition because it was a timely and vigorous refutation of the charge that Jesus was allied with the devil—Jesus had decidedly rejected any pact with the evil one.

The temptation story as preserved to us in Matthew (and Luke), is a work of a literary type with a definite tendency. But its present form dates back to an older and more popular story of which a fragment is preserved in Mark 1:12f. We can no longer establish with certainty the story originally told of Jesus' sojourn in the desert. If it is accurate that we must set the third temptation of Matt. and Luke here, then *temptations* would be at issue and not any conflict (cf. Bultmann, *The History of the Syn-*

optic Tradition, New York, 1963, p. 255f.). The action took place, whether in the desert where the beasts played a certain role, or on a high mountain, and the whole of it lasted forty days. The angels who came to serve him (Matt. 4:11), originally formed part of the ancient tradition.[30]

HEALING AND THE FORGIVENESS OF SINS: MARK 2:1-12

The story of the healing of the paralytic at Capernaum belongs to the genre of "controversies." The scene is described with much animation. All obstacles are overcome in order to bring the sick man to Jesus. Jesus gives him the assurance of the forgiveness of his sins and the narrative, after brief and dramatic defense against adversaries, closes with Jesus' triumph and the healing of the sick man.

The structure of the episode brings to mind other, similar fragments of the tradition where we find the same scheme. Nevertheless, the pericope of the paralytic offers certain features which suggest that it is not preserved in its original form, but that it has undergone some alterations, one of which makes especially clear primitive Christianity's judgment of miracle.

Critics have expressed surprise at seeing Jesus openly declare here that he was the Son of man invested with full powers to forgive sins on earth. This attitude does not correspond to that customarily adopted by Jesus toward the public in Mark. Only after Peter's confession (Chap. 8), and only in communication with his disciples does Jesus give himself the title ὁ υἱὸς τοῦ ἀνθρώπου. Then, expecting to find the term "man" in the antonymn of εἷς ὁ θεός (vs. 7), the exegetes conclude that the original text contained the words οἱ υἱοὶ τῶν ἀνθρώπων (= οἱ ἄνθρωποι in Mark 3 :28; cf. Matt. 9 :8). Contrary to the meaning of the original, the translator would then have replaced these words with the title ordinarily given only the Messiah (cf. G. Dupont, *Le fils de l'homme,* Paris, 1924, pp. 41ff.).

But the real problem is to be sought elsewhere, and the proposed solution just mentioned is unlikely and superfluous. For Mark 2 :1ff. is a miscellany of a number of episodes which are similar enough in nature and style that if in one of them Jesus publicly proclaims he is Messiah, it would not deter the evangelist from adding this piece to his collection, though it really does not suit his scheme. Then the adjunct "God alone" is not any man at all, but precisely the "Son of man," for here it is a case of Jesus' powers and celestial dignity. This pericope must then be examined separately, without accounting for the whole of the evangelist's composition.

But then we cannot resist the very distinct impression that in its present form the narrative has been greatly altered. Bultmann *(The History of the Synoptic Tradition,* pp. 14ff.) has shown that the controversy in vss. 5b-10 is inserted into the original healing narrative, for vs. 11 is the natural conclusion to a miracle story and tells us nothing of the impression made on adversaries, but only on spectators. A second observation serves to corroborate this opinion. When Jesus moves from forgiveness to healing he is prompted by his adversaries' *reflections* which he "perceived in his spirit." The scribes do not utter a word, yet the narrator is quite accurately informed on their thoughts: "Why does this man speak thus? It is blasphemy! Who can forgive sins but God alone?" The words of Jesus which follow are a direct reply to this tacit objection. This is undoubtedly a stylized literary form. It is true that elsewhere we are told of Jesus' reply to his opponents' unspoken censure (e.g., in 3:1ff.), but in this case the criticism results from the particular situation (healing on the sabbath).

The secondary character of our pericope is also indicated by application of the title ὁ υἱὸς τοῦ ἀνθρώπου to this specific situation. The exact parallel is found in Mark 2:28, "so the Son of man is lord even of the sabbath." This phrase which concludes the fragment quite inappropriately follows the speech which precedes it, "the sabbath was made for man, not man for the sabbath" (vs. 27). For better or worse, the redactor evidently intends to connect everything to Jesus in order to establish his authority. In its present form, the pericope of the paralytic pursues the same goal.

It must also be noted that this is the only time in the synoptic tradition that the question of the *forgiveness of sins* is raised. This fact leads us to think that a very current subject in the church has been introduced into an ordinary healing narrative. In this connection, Bultmann states that this pericope "has manifestly arisen from the dispute about the right (ἐξουσία) to forgive sins, a right which is to be attested by the power to heal miraculously"

(The History of the Synoptic Tradition, p. 15). This is a judicious remark, and it is proper to take our stance from this point of view in order to understand the present narrative in its present form.

The spokesmen for faith in Christ announced the ἄφεσις τῶν ἁμαρτιῶν to those who believed in the crucified and risen Christ. But certainly they also gave assurance of the forgiveness of sins to each repenting sinner, referring this power back to Jesus himself (Matt. 18:18). When the Jews reproached them for having usurped a right reserved to God alone and accused them of blasphemy, they had to indicate the source from which the master who had sent them derived his powers. He is the author of this practice and justified it by his acts. The deed of Jesus recorded in Mark 2:1ff. is the prototype which also legitimizes his disciples' later activity.

Our pericope is of particular interest from this specific point of view and shows us the value primitive Christianity assigned to miracle.

To prove ἐξουσία by miracle was completely consonant with the spirit of primitive Christianity and of antiquity in general. But the story of the paralytic does not immediately give proof by miracle. Beforehand, Jesus utters some very curious and interesting words: "Which is easier, to say to the paralytic, 'Your sins are forgiven,' or to say, 'Rise, take up your pallet and go home?'" Exegetes are highly embarrassed by these words (vs. 9). Ordinarily, they are explained by the Jewish idea of an essential connection between sin and sickness (John 9:1ff.), and in our pericope forgiveness and healing are viewed as two acts of the same drama. Hence,

to the question, Which is easier, to forgive or to
heal? the answer must be that both are alike. Whoever has power to do the one is also able to do the
other.

But the healing is neither to complete nor to perfect the forgiveness; it is to prove Jesus' spiritual
power. The miracle draws its conclusive force from
its own nature, not from an intrinsic connection
between sin and sickness. Jesus could just as well
have given another sign to prove his divine power,
but in these circumstances healing was required. If
the answer to the question, Which is easier? was
only that both are equally easy, and whoever has
power to do the one is able to do the other, the
affirmation of Jesus would be a truism. We cannot
rest with such an explanation.

We could sooner admit the opinion expressed by
E. Klostermann, that Jesus enters the thought of the
scribes and recognizes that it is easy, in effect, to
give assurance of forgiveness because it is impossible to verify whether forgiveness is actually
granted. But if Jesus does the hardest thing by
healing the paralytic, then what is easiest is proved
by implication. But then we should not expect a
(ἵνα) δὲ, but rather an οὖν (vs. 10). Further, this
explanation exaggerates the importance of εἰπεῖν,
Which is easier to *say* . . . ? But the "say," of course,
already includes the deed. One could as well have
written, What is easier to do, to forgive sins or to
heal?

Actually, the tone of the words in vs. 9 is *polemical*. To get a clear idea of this we need only examine
vs. 10 (ἵνα δὲ εἰδῆτε . . .) which is easily connected

with the words of reproof in vs. 8. ("why do you question thus in your hearts?"). Verse 9 is an interpolation, arising from another spiritual milieu than that which, true to its notions, set forth Jesus' triumph over his enemies by means of healing. The issue here is of a man for whom forgiveness is the real miracle, whereas the healing is secondary, i.e., proof in face of unbelief—in short, something inferior. The question is pitted against the traditional idea that miracle legitimates spiritual power. Our redactor feels a profound aversion for this entirely vulgar reasoning, and at bottom draws a conclusion *a minore ad maius*. Jesus' enemies, however (and most believers), reason the other way around. It is good, then, to rebut them in this way.

As a result, we have here a spiritual aristocrat who raises his voice in the midst of our popular narrative to utter words of a scarcely veiled irony. In vs. 9, we hear a man of the spiritual family of Paul, that great aristocrat of primitive Christianity who, after begging the Lord three times to heal him, received the reply, "my grace is sufficient for you" (2 Cor. 12:9).

The final redactor of our pericope cavils at this narrative. But without rejecting the tradition he adds a new feature which in the context of the narrative expresses his personal thought. In general, this is the method of primitive Christianity. Extremism was repugnant to it; its inner religious power adapted itself to the coexistence of frightful contrasts which inevitably branched off later on. Purism certainly merits esteem, but it is not the less sterile and petty. What superiority and refinement of mind, content, with a touch of subtle irony, to take up a tradition which is antipathetic to it, and which without it would only be vulgar and banal!

LIMITATION ON THE VALUE OF MIRACLE

Let us first examine the tiny pericope in Luke 10:17-20:

> The seventy returned with joy, saying, "Lord, even the demons are subject to us in your name!" And he said to them, "I saw Satan fall like lightning from heaven. Behold, I have given you authority to tread upon serpents and scorpions, and over all the power of the enemy; and nothing shall hurt you. Nevertheless do not rejoice in this, that the spirits are subject to you; but rejoice that your names are written in heaven."

The nucleus around which this pericope is crystallized is Jesus' speech which concludes it at vs. 20: "Do not rejoice. . . ." The accent is on these words. What precedes is only to set them in relief. All information on the situation converges at this point— the seventy, whose sending has just been related, return μετὰ χαρᾶς, triumphantly declaring that even the demons submitted to them. When Jesus sent them, demons were out of the question; he had commanded them to heal the sick (10:9; in 9:1, however, demons are expressly mentioned on the occasion of the sending of the twelve). Hence the disciples were greatly surprised to discover that even the demons were subject to them. That this is a characteristic feature taken from life itself cannot be doubted. As by chance, and to their own amazement, many discovered their capacity to heal and to exorcise demons.

Jesus' response amounts to a severe warning (10:20). For we must naturally consider this speech apart from Luke's composition. Taken alone, it is no less cutting, but it is not necessary to see in it a polemic against miracles. It only serves sternly and explicitly to relegate thaumaturgy to second rank. The entire emphasis is on the ἐν τούτω (μὴ χαίρετε) given first position. But the μὴ χαίρετε does not denote an absolute prohibition, only a relative one.

Thus Luke's interpretation is completely fair, whether this word harks back to Jesus himself or is of later origin. Luke has created the situation which forms the concrete background against which this peremptory word of Jesus stands out. It is presented as a response to the disciples' story on their return. But Luke wanted to develop this brief and concise response so as to secure its exact interpretation. In order to avoid any mistaken notion that Jesus on principle intended to deny the value of miracle, this reply is preceded by a few words of Jesus which sanction and confirm miracles. He had already learned that the disciples were casting out demons and took the keenest interest in their exorcisms: A vision causes him to see Satan fall from heaven (vs. 18). He then declares he has given them a *perpetual* authority over all the power of the enemy (vs. 19). Note the perfect active δέδωκα, which does not reflect this particular mission, but in general refers to missionaries' power to perform miracles. Thus the conclusion (vs. 20) clearly appears as a warning to the church not to attach too great importance to the miraculous.

This phrase has an ancient cast to it and expresses the mentality of primitive Christianity. First as to form, we are struck by a construction reminiscent of the Semitic phrase. Basically, the positive and negative commands are not at all incompatible, but express two different degrees of their respective worth which, thanks to a syntax imitative of Semitic languages, appears as a contrast of opposites. The spirit animating this speech appears in the words χαρά and χαίρειν. *Joy* was one of the characteristic traits of the ancient messianic church, joy in possessing salvation, joy in celebrating the cultus, joy in suffering. Many words in the New Testament are permeated with this spirit (Luke 6:23; 24:41; Acts 2:46; 5:41; 11:23; 13:52, etc.; cf. the Pauline triad: love, joy and peace). Our passage is a warning to all whose naive delight, excited by the miracles, leads them to extremes. There must be rejoicing, but this joy has its deep foundation in the blessed certainty that our names are written in heaven and that we belong to the elect. Here again we detect a truly ancient type speech which conforms to the usage of the Jewish language.

We see, then, that before long parenesis had to occupy itself with extraordinary phenomena in the church's life. The attitude toward miracle is completely positive, without being everywhere and always the same. The apostle Paul was confronted with a similar problem. But because the circumstances were different in his churches, they needed to be treated differently. Paul did not encounter that naive and overflowing joy which the miracles occasioned, and so it was enough to focus on the profoundest and most serious motif—complete joy. His task was to set aright an enthusiastic, excited, extremely presumptuous and even exacting movement. Here the notion of love *intervenes,* the first element in his great triad, a notion developed in a celebrated chapter of 1 Corinthians.

1 CORINTHIANS 13

In our research on the tendency limiting the influence of miracle in the New Testament, we could not neglect this essential text. It is true that miracles properly so called are not involved, but rather spiritual gifts. Still, among the χαρίσματα or πνευματικά enumerated in Chapter 12, we also find the χαρίσματα ἰαμάτων and ἐνεργήματα δυνάμεων. In general, this chapter is dominated by a critical spirit, fairly analogous to what we believed we uncovered in the preceding paragraph.

In this epistle to the Corinthians, it is no longer *salvation* which is prized as the highest gift, towering over all other manifestations and righting excesses provoked by the joy of working or seeing miracles—now it is love (ἡ ἀγάπη). Even though highly prizing the *charismata,* the apostle sees himself led by the turn of events at Corinth to assign them only limited value, and in contrast to attach greatest importance to the most essential of the great Christian virtues—love.

Why does he specifically mention love? First, no

doubt, because Jesus himself had called love of
neighbor the greatest commandment. Later, Paul
himself in Rom. 13:10 speaks of it as the fulfillment
of the law, thus setting love at the center of that
very law (we might reflect on the importance which
the apostle, the one-time Pharisee, assigned the
law). Love, as he explicitly puts it, is the greatest
virtue of the three: faith, hope and love. But it must
be said that the state of mind in the church at
Corinth required that love be shown to be an indispensable virtue. Already the arrogance of *gnosis*
toward those less enlightened, provoked these other
words in 8:1: "Knowledge puffs up, but love builds
up." But if it is easy to understand that Paul wanted
to lead those who boasted of their spiritual gifts to
an examination of conscience by referring them to
love as the greatest of virtues, 1 Cor. 13 still offers
exegesis a series of problems which in part still
await solution.

What is first striking is that this fragment on
love, self-contained both in substance and form,
appears in the midst of an account of the *charismata*
and obviously interrupts the sequence of Chapters
12-14. The words in 14:1b—μᾶλλον δὲ (ἵνα προφητεύητε
—could be connected to 12:31a—ζηλοῦτε δὲ τὰ χαρίσματα
τὰ μείζονα—without leaving a gap, but 12:31b and
14:1 appear to be most clumsily placed expletives.
For the moment, we will forego any conjecture regarding the text, for it is the content which interests
us here. But in the exposition which follows, we
cannot entirely omit questions relative to style and
form.

In a critical study undertaken on 1 Cor. 13 and

published in *Theologische Studien und Kritiken* in 1922 (pp. 54ff.), I felt it necessary to challenge the authenticity of this chapter. I considered Chapter 13 an interpolation made by an opponent of the spiritual gifts—someone of Stoic tendency who opposed moral self-discipline to unbridled enthusiasm. What enticed me at first was the relationship M. Edv. Lehmann's penetrating analysis revealed between the description of love in our chapter and the Stoic moral ideal (cf. E. Lehmann, *Stället och vägen*, Stockholm, 1917, p. 283f.), an observation I was able to complete by furnishing proof of a striking resemblance with Stoic terminology and style (cf. C. Clemen, *Religionsgeschichtliche Erklärung des Neuen Testaments*, 2nd edition, Giessen, 1924, pp. 326-329). Then I thought I had proved that at certain key points, Chapter 13 contradicted other Pauline ideas, especially his concept of ἀγάπη and estimation of *gnosis*.

Concerning *agape* in the study above mentioned (p. 63 f., *supra*) I formulated the problem thusly:

For Paul, *agape* is one of the Christian virtues alongside joy, peace and long-suffering (Gal. 5:22). For our author, it is *the* virtue par excellence, producing all the others.

Paul's *agape* is oriented to social action; that of our author is an act of individual and moral preservation by inner discipline.

The *agape* of Paul results in an intensification of feeling; 1 Cor. 13 sees in love only the mastery of feeling.

The solution enabling us to avoid this difficulty is to omit from a definition of *agape* what 1 Cor. 13

says about love, and to see there a typical *ad hoc,* directed against the schemings of the Corinthian Gnostics. In effect, the content of vss. 4-7 tends to corroborate this viewpoint. What we read there of ἀγάπη does not set forth its very essence, but assigns it various qualities which apply to the particular situation the letter depicts. Indeed, the words take a more general turn at the end (vs. 7), but I have demonstrated that this whole development reduces itself to a figure of rhetoric and a declamatory style, which require alternation of negative and affirmative (οὐ . . . πάντα; cf. Maximus Tyrius Philosophoumena, ed. Hobein, XX2).

But, from the standpoint of composition, can we explain how it happens that a self-contained fragment, arranged so exactly according to the rules of rhetoric, should appear in midst of this long, connected discourse on the *charismata?* Must we not rather suppose that a hymn to love, a hymn-fragment on *agape,* already self-contained and fixed in form, was inserted here? Then the 13th Chapter would not be composed *ad hoc,* but would explain a principle, and the objection which we have raised would be well founded. But I believe it is possible to see in this chapter an integral part of the composition of 1 Corinthians, if we explain the singular place it occupies in the context of Chapters 12-14 by a use frequent in antiquity, viz., *digression* (παρέκβασις). This is an idea I cannot develop here, and so will be content to refer the reader to Ed. Norden's *Die antike Kunstprosa* (p. 80), and especially to R. Kukula's preface to the translation of Tatian's apology *(Bibliothek der Kirchenväter,* I,

Kempten, 1913). *Digression* is mainly used in three ways: 1) as a lyrical exuberance; 2) for variation, and 3) in place of annotation. For Chapter 13, the first and second types come into consideration. Without going so far as to say that Paul had enjoyed a formal rhetorical education, in regard to this chapter we must still assign him some knowledge of the laws of rhetoric and the means available to it (cf. my earlier study mentioned above, p. 140 *supra*). We should not ignore the polemical and parenetic outline in 1 Cor. 13:1-7. In this case we will not hesitate to charge the rather awkward connectives in 12:31b and 14:1a to the apostle's account.

But we must still say a few words about γνῶσις. The apostle values it highly; he considers himself especially privileged, for though he is unskilled in speaking, he is not at all in *gnosis* (2 Cor. 11:6). Nevertheless, in 1 Cor. 13 he declares that our *gnosis* is only an imperfect knowledge (ἐκ μέρους γινώσκομεν, 13:9), and that one day it will be done away and replaced by the vision face to face (καταργηθήσεται, 13:8). In what, then, does this γνῶσις consist? The apostle clearly distinguishes between γνῶσις, σοφία, and προφητεία (ᾧ μὲν . . . δίδοται λόγος σοφίας, ἄλλῳ δὲ λόγος γνώσεως . . . . ἄλλῳ [δὲ] προφητεία, 12:8ff.; ἢ ἐν ἀποκαλύψει ἢ ἐν γνώσει ἢ ἐν προφητείᾳ, 14:6). Prophecy proceeds from sudden illumination, but *gnosis* and wisdom are qualities a man has in himself to greater or lesser degree, depending on the man. But what is the difference between γνῶσις and σοφία? Wisdom is the knowledge of divine things (τὰ τοῦ θεοῦ, 1 Cor. 2:11), especially the plan of salvation (τὰ ὑπὸ τοῦ θεοῦ χαρισθέντα ἡμῖν, 2:12; cf. θεοῦ σοφίαν . . . ἣν προώρισεν ὁ θεὸς πρὸ αἰώνων εἰς δόξαν ἡμῶν, 2:7). It not only perceives the entire history of redemption, but it also knows how the world was created and the universe is governed; it emerges as the Christian expression of the Jewish *chokmah*. The μυστήρια of the dispensation of grace (13:2: ἐὰν εἰδῶ τὰ μυστήρια πάντα) are the chief object of wisdom. A similar *mysterion* is revealed in 1 Cor. 15:51ff., and gives precise details concerning the resurrection of the dead and the transformation of the living at the parousia.

H. J. Holtzmann *(Neutestamentliche Theologie, 1911, I, pp. 553ff.)* defines the content of γνῶσις as the profoundest meaning of Scripture grasped in a moment of rapture, and states that it is identical to σοφία. This remark cannot be correct. Γνῶσις is distinguished from σοφία by a certain rational quality —it is really a "knowledge." It not only considers the given empirical reality (that goes without saying) but also embraces all that ancient man thought belonged to the domain of reality—demonology, for example (1 Cor. 8:4ff.).

It is truly remarkable that for practical reasons the apostle drew certain limits in 1 Cor. both for the propagation of σοφία and for the value of *gnosis*. It is instructive to compare these two parallel steps; wisdom clearly seems more valuable and attractive to him than *gnosis,* which he treats in a tone at times clearly reminiscent of polemic.

Paul speaks of wisdom in 1 Cor. 2:6—3:4. In what precedes this section, he emphasized the fact that he preached the gospel to the Corinthians as a paradox contrary to common opinion, without ele-

gance of style and philosophical argumentation
(οὐ καθ᾽ ὑπεροχὴν λόγου ἢ σοφίας, 2:1). Faith is not to be
based on the wisdom of men, but on the power of
God (2:5). Here is how the course of his argument
is to be interpreted: "It is true that there is also a
wisdom of God (σοφία θεοῦ, 2:6), but I have not told
you of it before because I reserve it ἐν τοῖς τελείοις
(exclusively)." Τέλειοι must be understood of Christians who are "grown men" (cf. the contrast νήπιοι
ἐν Χριστῷ in 3:1; 14:20; Phil. 3:15).[31] The detailed
account and explanation of the idea that he intends
to reserve wisdom for those who are "grown men"
is interrupted for a moment by a description of
σοφία. Only in 3:1 does Paul resume his account.
In passing he described God's wisdom as the precious privilege of the πνευματικοί (2:7-15). But are
not the Corinthians πνευματικοί? Here the apostle runs
into difficulty. The Christians of Corinth had and
still possess the πνεῦμα, but are immature from the
ethical point of view. Here Paul touches on a missionary experience which cannot easily be reconciled
with his theory of the Spirit as generative principle.
The Christians' possession of the Spirit and their
moral state often do not match. Paul then tells the
Corinthians that he has not been able to speak to
them *as* spiritual men (ὡς πνευματικοῖς) but *as* σάρκινοι.
He even goes so far as to call them σάρκινοι because
of their ζῆλος and ἔρις (3:3). Obviously, this remark
should be taken *cum grano salis*.[32] In principle, possession of the πνεῦμα was supposed to produce a perfect morality, but reality takes on another aspect—
the Corinthians, though elect, called and amply furnished with spiritual gifts, are still deeply entangled

in their human nature (ἄνθρωποί ἐστε, 3:4). Given their lack of spiritual maturity, σοφία would endanger their piety, for it would exceed their powers (οὔπω γὰρ ἐδύνασθε, 3:2). With what tact and finesse Paul alludes to the dangers of σοφία, whereas he brusquely and caustically says of γνῶσις that "knowledge puffs up" (8:1)!

There is more—γνῶσις is limited. The realm of knowledge is so vast each can know but a small part of it. That is why it is essential to knowledge to recognize that we do not know a great deal (8:2). This passage already anticipates the ἐκ μέρους of 13:8.

One of the most impressive traits of Paul's character is his energetic defense of pedagogical needs and the experiences of practical life against religious enthusiasm and speculation. In unparalleled fashion he combines incorruptible moral sobriety with a lofty flight of the spirit. A man solidly anchored in the ethical, he exhorts the faithful at Thessalonica, "do not quench the Spirit!" (1 Thess. 5:19). This is certainly a heritage which derives from Jesus and the primitive church. A remarkable document of this type of thought is preserved in 1 Cor. 13, and from this viewpoint we should consider it an integral part of the ideas set forth in Chapters 12-14.

The common interpretation of the sequence of ideas in this section is that Chapter 13 intends to emphasize prophecy which can be employed in the service of love as the best *charisma*. This is why we read μᾶλλον ἵνα προφητεύητε in 14:1. But this interpretation takes no account of the order in which the ideas follow each other. Prophecy has its own eminent value, is independent of love, and ἀγάπη is in no way linked to προφητεία. It is assumed there is a προφητεία without love. 1 Cor. 13 is a reaction of normal religious sentiment to the eccentricities and exaggerations of the Spirit. This is indicated by the encumbered and uneven phrase διώκετε τὴν ἀγάπην, ζηλοῦτε δὲ τὰ πνευματικά which refers us back to the main subject in 14.

We already established above that it is ἀγάπη which supplies a corrective. But perhaps we could go still further in our search for the origins of Chapter 13. If we consider the manifestations of the Spirit indicated by Paul in 13:1-3, we see that he combined heterogeneous elements—on the one hand, tongues, prophecy, mysteries, *gnosis* and faith (1-2); on the other, giving away all one's goods and the moral power to deliver one's body to be burned (3). The first group includes the *charismata,* the second acts for the good of the brethren (ἵνα καυθήσομαι, an obscure expression, no doubt alluding to the custom of branding and selling oneself as a slave in order to remit the purchase price to the church; cf. E. Preuschen, *Zeitschrift f. neutestl. Wissenschaft* XVI, 1915, pp. 127ff.). It appears from all we have just said that the counterpart and rival of ἀγάπη has its natural place in the *final* list of concepts and not in the first group which includes the *charismata.* In the matter of giving away one's wealth, etc., for good of the brethren, a contrast appears which is very striking because it is based on the very nature of things—*the purely outward, charitable act* versus *inner feeling.* Paul is surely calling to mind here a constant and fairly wide-spread feature of primitive Christian parenesis.[33]

In this general parenesis we must seek the origin of the development in 1 Cor. 13:1-3. Paul extends the *contrast* between *outward act* and *inner feeling* to the *charismata* as well. But then we must state that the two parts of the contrast do not exactly correspond. For *charismata* could not be compared with charitable acts. This is why scholars could ask if it were a matter of the love of God or of the brethren here. The problem is solved when we observe the starting point of the argument mentioned above. First, there is the contrast between outward charitable action and the inner love of the soul; then the charismatic deed, but without the indispensable moral base (here, ἀγάπη rather denotes "Christian character").

Paul's reservations on the subject of unbridled enthusiasm were just as precisely stated in regard to miracle's invasion of religion. The ἰάματα and δυνάμεις have their place among the *charismata;* they belong to the manifestations of the divine power. On this point as on others the apostle shared the conception peculiar to primitive Christianity. He was familiar with miracles as phenomena accompanying missionary work and performed some himself (cf. pp. 56 ff. *supra*). But we sense that the center of gravity for Paul's piety does not lie in thaumaturgy. For him, the greatest miracle is God's love for fallen and perverted humanity, and to define the gospel he uses the technical term which always denotes miracle—*dynameis* (Rom. 1:16). The fruits of the Spirit are the Christian virtues (Gal.

5:22). When the apostle himself is weak and harassed in the flesh by the devil, the grace of the Lord is sufficient for him (2 Cor. 12:7ff.). In Paul this attitude takes on the mark of a powerful individual originality and creates a spiritual bond which links him closely to the higher elements of the primitive church.

There was a chasm between charismatic virtuosity and moral value. This fact gave the apostle's conscience a pedagogical type problem. He tried to resolve it by way of serious and forceful exhortation. Time, moreover, came to his rescue. Little by little, enthusiasm died and ecclesiastical ethic alone took occupancy. His victory was perhaps more complete than Paul himself had wished. The Pastoral Epistles attest to this development; here everything falls in with the same dominant viewpoint, that of the true Christian life. The spirit of the great chapter on love no longer breathes through these words, and the imposing creative power which conceived this monumental digression was quenched.

Other dangers now menaced the church. There were believers who not only no longer knew how to unite spiritual gifts with the inner cultivation of religion, but also publicly put miracle to dishonest use.

THE FALSE PROPHETS

"Beware of false prophets, who come to you in sheep's clothing but inwardly are ravenous wolves. You will know them by their fruits." We already find this solemn warning in Jesus' mouth in the

Sermon on the Mount (Matt. 7:15ff.). Who were these false prophets? We have here a brief description of their character: They settle down nowhere but go here and there, from one church to another (ἔρχονται πρὸς ὑμᾶς) viewing the prophetic gift as a source of gain (λύκοι ἅρπαγες). We can specify the activity of these men still more exactly. They prophesy, exorcise demons, and perform miracles of all sorts in Jesus' name (7:22).

The pericope begins with a *warning* (7:15) and a *rule* on how to recognize false prophets (vs. 16). This last thought is developed in vss. 16b-18, 20, in which a well-known motif is used. Next comes a *threat* (vss. 21-23; cf. vs. 19) which calls attention to the judgment: At that time a final sentence will expose the false prophets for what they are. If they invoke their miracles, it will be of no use, for they will be harshly repulsed—οὐδέποτε ἔγνων ὑμᾶς.

We see immediately that vss. 21-23 form a secondary fragment, a supplement joined to vss. 15-20. These verses (21-23) obviously transform and stylize older ideas and formulas. In 7:21 a general proposition prepares for an announcement of the fate awaiting false prophets at the moment of judgment: "Not everyone who says to me, 'Lord, Lord,' shall enter the kingdom of heaven." Just as can be deduced from the passage in Luke 6:46, the κύριε, κύριε is originally viewed as an outward sign of the worship given to Jesus. In Matthew, on the other hand, the souls summoned to the Messiah's tribunal cry, "Lord, Lord!" Luke 6:46 expresses the contrast between a purely external worship and genuine obedience. In Matthew this contrast is suppressed and the eschatological dominates. The redactor of this passage is not content with the simple rule that false prophets will be known by their "fruits" (vss. 7, 16-18, 20). He intends to address them with a *warning* which recalls the last judgment (vss. 19, 21-23). We note that not only vs. 21, but vss. 19 and 22f. as well are only imitations (on vs. 19, cf. Matt. 3:10, a word attributed to the Baptist; and on vs. 22f., cf. Luke 13:26ff.: "We ate and drank in your presence, and you taught in our streets. But he will say, 'I tell you, I do not know where you come from!' ").

Matt. 7:21-23 thus has only subordinate value. It uses and modifies several motifs and verses to serve notice on the false prophets. But the historical value of this passage and of the entire pericope in Matt. 7:15ff. is no less evident for all that. The pericope reflects a situation which could have existed in Syro-Palestinian churches around the year 80—greedy vagabonds claiming to be Christian prophets by performing miracles and prophesying in the name of Jesus.

It is true that the final redaction of Matthew's Sermon on the Mount regards our pericope as a general warning to *all* members of the church to be on guard against false show (cf. the rubric in K. Aland, *Synopsis Quattuor Evangeliorum*, 3rd edition, 1964, No. 74). The general theme which for him determines the sequence of ideas appears in the parable of the narrow and the wide gate, the hard and the easy way (7:13ff.). To enter by the narrow gate, to walk the hard way, is to live by doing God's will. The redactor also finds this general idea in the

passage on false prophets. This is why he set these
words here. But what is important for us is the
original meaning of our pericope which is perfectly
clear: The reference is not to Christians of whatever kind, but to persons of a quite peculiar class—
the pseudo-prophets.

Let us examine more closely the notion of false
prophet given in our text. What type of persons were
these false prophets, and in the judgment of Matt.
7:15-22? Clearly, they are portrayed as men without conscience, hypocrites, who under pretext of
piety work miracles for their own profit. In this
respect, our pericope discloses a primitive outlook—
Jesus' name has a magical power which even imposters and magicians can use.[34] The anecdote related in Mark 9:38ff. is an interesting example
which illustrates this idea. It enjoins tolerance to-
wards exorcists who operate outside the church,
invoking the name of Jesus. The narrative in Acts
19:14ff. of the ignominy visited on the sons of
Sceva, one of the high priests, relates a similar
deed, but manifests a less tolerant spirit. When a
thaumaturge disguises himself as a Christian prophet, he becomes a danger to the church which must
defend itself against him. The danger consists not
only in being deceived and exploited, but also in
suffering the pernicious influence of such a man.
He is an active liquidator of the religious life; he
has something of the demonic, is an ἐργαζόμενος τὴν
ἀνομίαν.

The notion of *anomia* is not without importance
for an understanding of the early Christian idea of
the false prophet. In the Septuagint, the term is

regularly used to translate *eben* (cf. Psalms 91 and 93, LXX), and S. Mowinckel has shown that in the Psalms the "doers of *eben*" (οἱ ἐργαζόμενοι τὴν ἀνομίαν) are originally sorcerers who, by means of magical powers, work all sorts of noisome influences *(Psalmenstudien* I, Oslo, 1921). We also find ἀνομία, ἀνομέω, ἀνόμημα and ἄνομος in the magical papyri, where these words denote those who oppose divine laws by seeking to pervert them (cf. *Papyri Osloënses* I, ed. Eitrem, 1925, 141; cf. the commentary on pp. 65ff.; Pap. Mag. Par., ed. Wessely, *Denkschriften der kais. Akademie der Wissenschaften,* Hist. phil. Klasse XXXVI, Wien, 1888, 1776, 3099; Pap. Mimaut ibid., p., 142, 87; H. Audollent, *Defixionum Tabellae,* Paris, 1904, Nr. 155, 188). In 2 Thess. 2:3-9, Paul predicts the revelation (ἀποκάλυψις) of the ἄνθρωπος τῆς ἀνομίας, ὁ ἄνομος, τὸ μυστήριον τῆς ἀνομίας:

> Unless the rebellion comes first, and the man of lawlessness is revealed, the son of perdition, who opposes and exalts himself against every so-called god or object of worship, so that he takes his seat in the temple of God, proclaiming himself to be God. . . . The coming of the lawless one by the activity of Satan will be with all power and with pretended signs and wonders, and with all wicked deception for those who are to perish.

In this passage, the term ἀνομία has an eschatological import (cf. ἀποκάλυψις) with the result that "lawlessness" expands to enormous proportions. But basically it is the same diabolical ἐνέργεια which is at work, though more discreetly, in the activity of the false prophet. In his primitive, popular form, this prophet is of an entirely *practical* cast. He intends to satisfy his lusts by using any and all means— magic, Jesus' name, malefices.

Such persons I believe were originally intended in the parable of the tares among the wheat (Matt. 13:24ff., 37ff.). The ζιζάνια, children of Satan, sown by the devil; the σκάνδαλα, οἱ ποιοῦντες τὴν ἀνομίαν are the false prophets. The evangelist perhaps interpreted these terms in a larger, broader sense, but the question originally treated in the parable was, must we try to drive false prophets from the church? And the reply was, no, for in so doing we might weed out the true. "Let both grow together until the harvest!" Naturally, this does not prevent being on one's guard—precisely what Matt. 7:15ff. advises by referring to the last judgment.[35]

There is variety in the New Testament idea of the false prophet. In Matthew we located a *primitive type*, the thaumaturge and ecstatic who works his miracles in Jesus' name for his own profit. Such are the charlatans, who, however, are unmasked by their evil conduct.

Another type of false prophet is the false *teacher*, an instrument of the devil to mislead the faithful from the truth. Paul calls his opponents at Corinth ψευδαπόστολοι,[36]

> deceitful workmen, disguising themselves as apostles of Christ. And no wonder, for even Satan himself is disguised as an angel of light. So it is not strange if his servants also disguise themselves as servants of righteousness. Their end will correspond to their deeds (2 Cor. 11:13-15).

Here the term "false" is subjective in tone, but later on the word ψεύδοη becomes a part of ecclesiastical terminology and is used in polemic against the *heretics* (1 John 4:1; cf. ψευδοδιδάσκαλοι 2 Peter 2:1).

A particular type of false prophet belongs to *eschatology*. This type will emerge when the end comes, and will lead many astray by miracles, so that they abandon God and Christ (Mark 13:22; Matt. 24; Rev. 16-20; cf. 2 Thess. 2).[37]

We note that however varied the genre of false prophets, polemic always employs the same features and motifs. The following characteristic feature, strikingly expressed by the λύκοι ἄρπαγες in Matt. 7, is always underscored—false prophets are out to make money so as to live at ease (cf. 2 Peter and the Pastoral Epistles). Then comes the *warning:* They will be known by their fruits, and the *threat:* "Their end will correspond to their deeds." [38]

A generation later, in the *Didache* (Chap. XI) and *Hermas* (Mand. XI), we meet in more developed form that original type of false prophet we learned to know from Matt. 7. Here, as in the Gospel, the thought is not of propagating this or that false doctrine, but simply of exercising prophecy (instructions, warnings, and prophecies in the form of ecstatic discourse). In the Didache and Hermas, neither healings of demoniacs nor miracles are involved, though they are not lacking. *Lucian,* on the death of Peregrinus 11-13, 16, vividly describes a similar false prophet: Proteus passes himself off as a prophet and leader of the assemblies; he explains the Holy Scriptures, composes some himself, is venerated as much as a god, and is the lawgiver

and director of the church. He receives gifts and
money in abundance. In Hermas and the Didache
the moral attitude distinguishes the false from the
true prophet:

> But not every one that speaketh in the Spirit is a
> prophet; but only if he hold the ways of the Lord.
> Therefore, from their ways shall the false prophet
> and the prophet be known (Didache XI, 8; cf.
> Hermas, Mand. XI, 7: Try the man who has the
> divine Spirit by his life). *(The Ante-Nicene Fa-
> thers,* VII, 380; II, 27).

Above all, it must be determined whether this man
is disinterested in profit and livelihood. The Didache
demonstrates this by a typical example.

The rationalist Lucian calls Christian prophets of
the Proteus Peregrinus sort (and, in short, all
prophets) charlatans and impudent mountebanks
(cf. 13 to the end: γόης καὶ τεχνίτης ἄνθρωπος καὶ πράγμασι
χρῆσθαι δυνάμενος). From the religious point of view,
the judgment had to be modified somewhat. The
naive idea in Matt. 7 that the power to work miracles was inherent in the name of Jesus grew in-
adequate to the extent false prophecy adopted sub-
tler forms. No doubt, Christian charlatans were in
large measure inspired by pagan thaumaturgy.
Moreover, superstitution and especially the mania
for consulting oracles—the order of the day in a
pagan milieu—penetrated the churches. We read
even in Hermas that the false prophet was considered a clever charlatan (Mand. XI, 2-3), and was
compared to the magician who, consulted on the
future, gives his questioners the answer they want
to hear, "and fills their souls with expectations,

according to their own wishes." In addition, we find
the idea that the false prophet is inspired by *the
devil:*

> Some true words he does occasionally utter; for the
> devil fills him with his own spirit, in the hope
> that he may be able to overcome some of the righ-
> teous. *(The Ante-Nicene Fathers,* II, 27).

We note that the problem of miracle always grew
more complicated because of the prophets' corrup-
tion, so that a man was never very sure he was in
the presence of a true or false prophet. The believers' discernment deteriorated and there was a penchant for a type of Christian magic. This is a fact
we can verify in Hermas. He calls those who run
after false prophets men of doubt, whose faith is
unsteady:

> As many, then, as are strong in the faith of the
> Lord, and are clothed with truth, have no connec-
> tion with such spirits, but keep away from them;
> but as many as are of doubtful minds and frequent-
> ly repent, betake themselves to soothsaying, even
> as the heathen, and bring greater sin upon them-
> selves by their idolatry. For he who inquires of a
> false prophet in regard to any action is an idolater,
> and devoid of the truth, and foolish (XI, 4; *The
> Ante-Nicene Fathers,* II, 27).

Thus false prophets threatened sound religious
life from without and within. It is no surprise,
therefore, that church leaders tried to suppress
miracles and prophecy.

We hear a distant echo of this problem in the
Apostolic Constitutions, drafted around the year
400. The eighth book of this work is based upon
a writing of Hippolytus now lost to us. At the out-

set, Hippolytus accounted for spiritual gifts (περὶ χαρισμάτων), the object of the discussion in the *Constitutions*, VIII, 1-2. Unfortunately, it is not certain that the redactor of the Constitutions really made use of the Hippolytus fragment. Still, the instructions which he placed in the mouth of the apostles were undoubtedly not invented *ad hoc*, but represent an opinion gradually formed over the years in areas of church government.[39]

In the course of the 250 years separating the Didache from the Apostolic Constitutions, primitive Christianity was transformed and became the church catholic. Enthusiasm disappeared, the ministry, cultus, and the moral law became the decisive factors in the church. We see how far the situation we meet in the Constitutions is removed from that of early Christianity in the fact that the *charismata* are denied any value to the church (i.e. τὰ χαρίσματα τὰ διὰ σημείων, θαυματοποιεῖν). They have value only for *unbelievers* [40] who will not allow the preaching to persuade them. And not even miracles influence everyone, but only the εὐγνώμονες. Religious life in the church does not have to do with miracles, but is totally regulated by cultus and morals. This sudden change in religious attitude is also seen in the oft-repeated affirmation that miracles are exclusively God's gift, whereas piety and thus salvation depend upon our will and zeal (εὔνοια καὶ σπουδή), "naturally, with the help of God." Hence miracles do not contribute to our salvation because, independent of our will, they do not constitute a *meritum*.

But the real purpose of this account is to guard against vanity and presumption. The spiritual man has no right to exalt himself above him who has not received the gift of the Spirit. Neither the bishop is to be elevated above elders and deacons, nor elders and deacons above the laity: τὸ μὲν εἶναι χριστιανοὶ ἐφ' ἡμῖν, τὸ δὲ ἀπόστολον ἢ ἐπίσκοπον ἢ ἄλλο . . . οὐκ ἐφ'ἡμῖν ἀλλ' ἐπὶ τῷ διδόντι θεῷ τὰ χαρίσματα.[41] The warning and interpretation are addressed as much to the χαρίσματα as to the ἀξιώματα (1:22). But what was the real importance of the *charismata* in the church of this epoch?

They no longer played any role in the church, and the term could very well have been lost, had not certain efforts to revive thaumaturgy emerged. Of course, these tendencies must be sought among the monks where enthusiasm reappeared along with miracle. But ecclesiastical authorities approved of this impulse only with the greatest reserve. The purpose of miracle is to propagandize; beyond this it could be suppressed. It is no longer a constitutive part of piety, but is still a supplementary gift of God which may not be vaunted. Whoever prophesies is not always a pious man, and whoever casts out demons is not always a saint (2:1). Even the impious can fill this role, as Balaam's example shows. But these reflections ought not discredit true prophecy (2:7); the intention is merely to expel and warn braggarts. The conclusion to this argument is that:

> It is not therefore necessary that every one of the faithful should cast out demons, or raise the dead, or speak with tongues; but such a one only who is vouchsafed this gift, for some cause which may be advantage to the salvation of the unbelievers, who

are often put to shame, not with the demonstration
of the world, but by the power of the signs; that
is, such as are worthy of salvation (VIII, 1, 4;
The Ante-Nicene Fathers, VII, 479).

This is language different from that of 1 Corinthians: "Earnestly desire the higher gifts." In the
great church the source of miracles was on the
point of drying up. Though it has never completely
run dry in the church catholic, it does flow between
the banks of faith and superstition. Enthusiasm as
the essential characteristic of the church's life is
dead forever and support for miracle has fallen
with it.[42]

Enthusiasm was destined gradually to disappear;
psychologically such a development was inescapable.
At the very outset complications loomed up and
produced a critical attitude toward miracle. It is
this state of mind and all it implies which we have
tried to analyse in the preceding chapters.

Notes

1. Among recent contributions to the discussion of miracle in general, we refer to the following studies: P. Saintyves, *Le discernement du miracle*, Paris, 1909; C. Gutberlet, *Vernunft und Wunder*, Munich, 1905; K. Beth, *Das Wunder*, Berlin, 1908; W. Herrmann, *Offenbarung und Wunder*, 1908; J. Wendland, *Der Wunderglaube im Christentum*, Tübingen, 1908; cf. *Zeitschrift für Theologie und Kirche* XXVI (1916) p. 231 ff.; F. Kattenbusch, "Über den Gedanken des Naturwunders," *Zeitschrift für Theologie und Kirche*, XXI (1911); H. Mandel, *Der Wunderglaube*, 1913; C. Stange, *Naturgesetz und Wunderglaube*, Leipzig, 1914; A. W. Hunzinger, *Das Wunder*, 1912; R. Paulus, "Zum religiösen Begriff des Wunders und der Natur," *Zeitschrift für Theologie und Kirche*, XXIV (1914); F. Traub, "Zur Wunderfrage," *Studien zur systematischen Theologie*, Theod. v. Häring dargebracht, Tübingen, 1918; W. Beyschlag, *Die Bedeutung des Wunders im Christentum*, 1863; R. Keubel, *Über den christlichen Wunderglaube*, 1883. On the miracles of the New Testament: Louis Menegoz, *La Notion biblique du miracle*, 1894; R. Wimmer, *Die biblischen Wundergeschichten*, Tübingen, 1890; W. Soltau, *Hat Jesus Wunder getan?* Leipzig, 1903; R. C. Trench, *Notes on the Miracles*, London, 15th ed., 1895; F. Ziller, *Die*

biblischen Wunder in ihrer Beziehung zu der biblischen Welt- und Gottesvorstellung, Tübingen, 1904 *(Sammlung gemeinverständlicher Vorträge* 38); K. Beth, *Die Wunder Jesu,* Berlin, 1905 *(Biblische Zeit- und Streitfragen* II, 1); L. Fonck, *Die Wunder des Herrn im Evangelium,* Innsbruck, 1907; G. Samtleben, *Die biblischen Wunder,* Gütersloh, 1907; Gottfr. Traub, *Die Wunder im Neuen Testament,* Tübingen, 1907 *(Religionsgeschichtliche Volksbücher* V, 2); P. Mehlhorn,*Wahrheit und Dichtung im Leben Jesu,* 2nd ed., 1911 *(Aus Natur und Geisteswelt);* J. M. Thompson, *Miracles in the New Testament,* London, 1911; A. C. Headlam, ʼ*The Miracles of the New Testament,* London, 1914; E. O. Davies, *The Miracles of Jesus,* London, 1913; J. R. Illingworth, *The Gospel Miracles,* London, 1916; R. Jelke, *Die Wunder Jesu,* Leipzig, 1924; Johannes Weiss in "Die Schriften des N. T. neu übersetzt und für die Gegenwart erklärt," 3rd ed., Göttingen, 1917, I, 50-56.

2. P. Fiebig, *Jüdische Wundergeschichten des neutestamentlichen Zeitalters,* Tübingen, 1911; *Rabbinische Wundergeschichten,* Bonn, 1911 (Lietzmann's *Kleine Texte* 78); A. Schlatter, *Das Wunder in der Synagogue (Beiträge zur Förderung christlicher Theologie* XVI, 5), Gütersloh, 1912); W. Ebstein, *Die Medizin im Neuen Testament und im Talmud,* 1903; R. Reitzenstein, *Hellenistischen Wundererzählungen,* Leipzig, 1906; Otto Weinreich, *Antike Heilungswunder, Religionsgeschichtliche Versuche und Vorarbeiten* VIII, 1, Giessen, 1909; P. Fiebig, *Antike Wundergeschichten,* Bonn, 1911 (Lietzmann's *Kleine Texte* 79); S. Herrlich, *Antike Wunderkuren,* Berlin, 1911; Ch. Blinkenberg, *Miraklerne i Epidauros,* Copenhagen, 1917; L. Trede, *Der Wunderglaube im Heidentum und in der alten Kirche,* 1901; R. Lembert, *Das Wunder bei den römischen Historikern, Jahresbericht des kgl. Realgymnasiums,* Augsburg, 1904; F. C. Baur, "Apollonios von Tyana und Christus," *Tübinger Zeitschrift für Theologie,* 1832; J. Hempel, *Untersuchungen zur Überlieferung von Apollonios von Tyana,* Leipzig, 1920; F. Pfister, *Der Reliquienkult im Altertum,*

I, Giessen, 1909 *(Religionsgeschichtliche Versuche und Vorarbeiten* V) ; J. Tambornino, *De antiquorum daemonismo,* Giessen, 1909 *(Religionsgeschichtliche Versuche und Vorarbeiten* VII, 3) ; J. Smit, *De daemoniacis in historia evangelica,* Rome, 1913; T. Taczak, *Dämonische Besessenheit,* Münster i. W., 1903; A. Titius, "Über Heilung von Dämonischen im Neuen Testament," *Festschrift für Bonwetsch, Leipzig,* 1918; K. Oesterreich, *Die Besessenheit,* Langensalza, 1921; E. R. Micklem, *Miracles and the New Psychology: A Study in the Healing Miracles of the New Testament,* Oxford, 1922; H. Rust, *Die Wunder der Bible,* I, 1922, II, 1923, Pfullingen i. Württ.

3. Regarding these interesting passages from Hebrews, cf. in addition to the remarks of H. Windisch (Lietzmann's *Handbuch,* 1913), E. Riggenbach *(Kommentar zum Neuen Testament,* ed. T. Zahn, 2nd ed., 1922) and J. Moffatt *(International Critical Commentary,* 1924), F. Buechsel, *Die Christologie des Hebräerbriefs,* Gütersloh, 1922 *(Beiträge zur Förderung christlicher Theologie* XXVII, 2). Buechsel thinks that the idea of Jesus' perfection through suffering is purely theological, or that it is logically developed as a consequence of the idea of Jesus as "Son of God." Against this view see E. F. Scott, *The Epistle to the Hebrews,* 2nd ed., Edinburgh, 1923.

4. The term *apomnemoneumata* applied to the Gospels (according to Xenophon's celebrated work on Socrates) is carefully examined by K. L. Schmidt in his important work, "Die Stellung der Evangelien in der allgemeinen Literaturgeschichte," *Festschrift Hermann Gunkel,* pp. 54ff. Schmidt justifiably rejects comparison with the literary genre of the *apomnemoneumata.* These latter belong to "haute littérature," whereas the Gospels belong to "petite littérature" *(Kleinliteratur).* Still, it must be recognized that the term *apomnemoneumata* as used of the Gospels was particularly intelligible to the educated Greek. In fact, when we recall Xenophon's memoirs, we are led to ask whether they do not bear some analogy to

the synoptics. It is not impossible that among the anecdotes told of Socrates, some hark back to an authentic,
popular tradition, to which Xenophon first gave literary
form. I owe this idea to my friend professor G. Rudberg.
According to him, examination of Xenophon's memoirs
with respect to a possible oral tradition is urgently
needed.

5. The most recent phase of synoptic criticism has already produced a considerable series of suggestive studies: M. Dibelius, *From Tradition to Gospel*, New York,
1965; K. L. Schmidt, *Der Rahmen der Geschichte Jesu*,
Berlin, 1919; *Die Stellung der Evangelien*, etc. (cf. the
preceding note); M. Albertz, *Die synoptischen Streitge-
spräche*, Berlin, 1921; R. Bultmann, *The History of the
Synoptic Tradition*, New York, 1963; G. Bertram, *Die
Leidensgeschichte Jesu und der Kyrioskult*, Göttingen,
1922. Not only in the conservative camp do we hear
criticisms of the theory these scholars advance: cf. E.
Aurelius, Till *frågan om den synoptiska traditionens
ursprung och älsta historia*, Lund, 1923; L. Brun, "Nye
veier i studiet av den evangeliske overlevering," *Norsk
Teologisk Tidskrift*, 1924, pp. 44ff. It was chiefly E.
Fascher who minutely examined these new points of
view in his study "Die formgeschichtliche Methode,"
(Beihefte zur *Zeitschrift für die neutestamentliche Wissenschaft* 2), Giessen, 1924. Fascher demonstrates that
the method known as "form criticism" is in its infancy;
it is far too one-sided and is not without exaggeration
and inner contradiction. In my opinion, we can at least
state certain permanently acquired results: a) the mania
for source analysis has been abandoned; b) the narrative
and the historical fact can no longer be naively identified,
since the popular and cultic character of most of the
synoptic tradition has been recognized, and the idea of
transmission by "eye-witnesses" has been given up; c)
the composition of the Gospel of Mark will be considered
from a literary, not a historical point of view; d) the
criteria of form and style will be taken into greater consideration than previously. On this subject, cf. the re-

marks of G. Baldensperger in *Revue de Théologie et de Philosophie* (Lausanne), 1924, pp. 180, 186, 189, 196.

6. As to the preface to Luke's Gospel, the interpretation of which, in all its parts, raises serious difficulties, cf. Henry J. Cadbury, "The Style and Literary Method of Luke," *Harvard Theological Studies* VI, 2 (1920) and in *The Beginnings of Christianity*, ed. F. J. Foakes-Jackson and Kirsopp Lake, I, 2, London, 1922, pp. 489-510; F. H. Colson and J. H. Ropes in the *Journal of Theological Studies* XXIV (1923), pp. 300ff., and XXV (1924), pp. 67ff.

7. For the idea of δύναμις see Julius Röhr, *Der okulte Kraftbegriff im Altertum, Philologus*, Supplement 17, 1, 1923; F. Preisigke, *Die Gotteskraft der frühchristlichen Zeit*, Berlin, 1922; *Vom göttlichen Fluidum*, Berlin, 1920; Ed. Meyer, *Ursprung und Anfänge des Christentums*, III, 1923, pp. 285ff.; T. Hopfner, *Griechisch-Aegyptischer Offenbarungszauber* II, Leipzig, 1924; H. Leisegang, *Die Gnosis*, Leipzig, 1924 (cf. the index under "Kraft").

8. The triad σημεῖα, τέρατα, δυνάμεις, is found in 2 Cor. 12:12; 2 Thess. 2:9, cf. Acts 2:22. Σημεῖα καὶ τέρατα: Rom. 15:19, cf. Heb. 2:4; Mark 13:22; John 4:48; Acts 2:43; 4:30; 5:12; 6:8; 7:36; 14:3; 15:12. Σημεῖα καὶ δυνάμεις: Acts 8:13. These various terms do not allow us to fix a differentiation or classification of miracles in primitive Christianity—they are stereotyped formulas.

9. For the meaning of the term πράξεις, cf. U. von Wilamowitz in *Die Kultur der Gegenwart*, I, 8, 3rd ed., 1912, p. 262. He finds this title perfectly suited to the second book *ad Theophilum*, in its present form. R. Reitzenstein, *Hellenistische Wundererzählungen*, p. 121f., and P. Wendland, *Die urchristlichen Literaturformen*, 3rd ed., Tübingen, 1912, pp. 315ff. For the contrary view, cf. A. von Harnack, *Beiträge zur Einleitung in das Neue Testament*, III, Leipzig, 1908, chapter 4; A. Wiken-

hauser, "Die Apostelgeschichte und ihr Geschichtswert" *(Neutestamentliche Abhandlungen,* published by M. Meinertz, VIII, 3-5), Münster i. W., 1921, pp. 96ff.

10. Christianity's hostile attitude toward magic is stressed in Ignatius, Adv. Ephe. 19, 3 (with Christ's birth, all magic has been abolished and every tie to wickedness destroyed); cf. Justin, Dial. 78, 7; Origen, Adv. Cels. I, 60; Tertullian, De Idol. 9; Barnabas 20:1; Didache 2:2; 5:1.

11. Gospel tradition in missionary preaching: A. Oepke, *Die Missionspredigt des Apostels Paulus,* Leipzig, 1920, pp. 132ff. (where we find the more ancient literature listed); K. Pieper, *Die Missionspredigt des heil. Paulus,* Paderborn, 1921, pp. 92ff.; M. Dibelius, *From Tradition to Gospel,* passim; cf. E. Fascher, *Die formgeschichtliche Methode,* pp. 78ff.; K. L. Schmidt, *Die Stellung des Apostels Paulus im Urchristentum* (Vorträge der theol. Konferenz zu Giessen 39), Giessen, 1924.

12. On εὐεργέτης as a title given the gods, cf. Pauly-Wissowa, *Realencyclopädie der class. Altertums* VI, 1909, p. 978f.

13. Whereas in Mark the deeper meaning of the entry into Jerusalem is hidden from the crowd, the same scene in Matthew is a publicly messianic demonstration. The crowd cries out, "Hosanna to the Son of David!" (21:9). Luke turns this episode into an homage given by the *crowd of disciples.* They begin to praise God in a loud voice for all the miracles they had seen and cried, "Blessed is the king who comes in the name of the Lord! Peace in heaven and glory in the highest!" (19:38). Neither Matthew nor Luke has sensed the unusual character of Mark's narrative; each has retouched this episode in his own way. A. Loisy *(l'Évangile selon Luc,* Paris, 1924, p. 149) believes he detects a particular tendency in Luke: Luke intends that Jesus be acknowledged as the Messiah (King), but not as presently establishing

his kingdom on earth. This is why the disciples praise God for all the wonders he has done. This is undoubtedly a fair observation (cf. Luke 17:20f.; Acts 1:6ff.). We note again that the expression of *joy* is emphasized (χαίροντες, cf. Luke 10:17).

14. An original idea on the mystery of Christ has been ventured by Chr. A. Bugge *(Das Christusmysterium,* Oslo, 1915, *Videnskapsselskapets skrifter,* II, Hist.-filos. Klasse, 1914, Nr. 3). Bugge thinks Jesus had already given his disciples an organization similar to the Essene type society of initiates into the mysteries *(Mysterien-gemeinde),* and that the μυστήρια τῆς βασιλείας represents the esoteric teaching of this group; cf. the recently published study by the same author, *Die älteste Kirchen-verfassung,* Oslo, 1924. I must forego mention of these interesting and wide-ranging ideas, which would require long and thorough study.

15. Regarding the most recent discussions on the subject of the "Messianic mystery" cf. R. Bultmann, W. Mundle, and E. Bickermann in *Zeitschrift für die neu-testamentliche Wissenschaft* XIX (1919-1920), pp. 165ff.; XXI (1922), pp. 299ff.; XXII (1923), pp. 122ff.

16. When Jesus' miracles are mentioned in the literature of early Christianity, it is almost always in the form of a *summary enumeration;* these passages are collected in E. Hennecke, *New Testament Apocrypha,* Philadelphia, 1965, Vol. I, p. 435. When it comes to an evaluation of the Lord's thaumaturgy, unity of outlook is lacking. Cf. W. Bauer, *Das Leben Jesu im Zeitalter der neutesta-mentlichen Apokryphen,* Tübingen, 1909, p. 365f.

17. How did Jesus himself judge his healings and exorcisms? On this question, cf. H. Monnier, *La mission his-torique de Jésus,* Paris, 1906, pp. 42-53; F. Barth, *Die Hauptprobleme des Lebens Jesu,* 3rd ed., Gütersloh, 1907, pp. 109-148; R. A. Hoffmann, *Die Erlösergedanken des geschichtlichen Christus,* Königsberg, 1911; R. Seeberg,

Der Ursprung des Christusglaubens, Leipzig, 1914, pp.
4ff.; A. von Harnack, *Mission und Ausbreitung des
Christentums,* 3rd ed., 1915, I, pp. 115-135; P. Wernle,
Jesus, Tübingen, 1916, pp. 284-287; for a detailed study,
cf. D. A. Frövig, "Das Sendungsbewusstsein Jesu und
der Geist" *(Beiträge zur Förderung christlicher Theologie,* XXIX, 3), Gütersloh, 1924. Frövig restates views
he had previously set forth. Cf. his work cited in note 1:
according to him, Jesus regarded his miracles as the
effect of the gift of the Spirit which properly belonged
to him. It seems to me this thesis far exceeds the truth,
and study of the sources does not give it serious support.
Obviously, we cannot deny the close connection between
the Spirit and miracle in the Jewish and early Christian
consciousness; cf. H. Gunkel, *Die Wirkungen des heilig-
en Geistes,* Göttingen, 1888; H. Weinel, *Die Wirkungen
des Geistes und der Geister,* Tübingen, 1899; but it is
not possible to establish that this view prevailed with
Jesus or the church. Luke, for whom the Spirit plays a
special role, often, but not always, sees in miracle the
effect of this Spirit (Luke 4:18; Acts 10:38; 13:9; A.
von Harnack, *Beiträge zur Einleitung,* III, p. 111f.).
Paul's thought is oriented in the same direction: 1 Cor.
12:9 and 11; 1 Thess. 1:5; Rom. 15:19; Gal. 3:5. But
this theory cannot be applied to all primitive Christianity, still less to Jesus. Wide-ranging conclusions cannot
be drawn from Matt. 12:28 because a) this passage is
quite unique in its genre; b) there is no unity in the
tradition (Luke 11:20); c) it is really doubtful that we
have an authentic speech of Jesus here, and d) ἐν πνεύματι
θεοῦ seems to be constructed in opposition to ἐν Βεελζεβούλ.
When it came to miracles, δύναμις was preferred to
pneuma (Luke 5:17; Acts 4:7; 1 Thess. 1:5), or to
δυνάμεις (Mark 6:14, cf. 5:30; Luke 6:19); πνεύματι ἁγίῳ
καὶ δυνάμει in Acts 10:38; 1 Cor. 2:4 has almost become a
fixed formula; similarly, χάρις καὶ δύναμις in Acts 6:8.
Ἐξουσία is a significant expression (Mark 1:27; 3:15;
6:7; Luke 10:19; Acts 8:19); ἐξουσία καὶ δύναμις in Luke
4:36; 9:1. These are the technical terms of thaumaturgic
language: ἐνέργεια, ἐνεργέω, ἐνέργημα in 2 Thess. 2:9; Mark

6:14; 1 Cor. 12:11; Gal. 3:5; 2 Thess. 2:7; 1 Cor. 12:6 and 10.

18. On the exorcisms of the early Christian Church, cf. A. von Harnack, *Mission und Ausbreitung des Christentums*, I, pp. 136-154.

19. The sign of the prophet Jonah, cf. J. H. Michael in the *Journal of Theological Studies* XXI (January 1920), pp. 146ff.; E. von Dobschütz, *The Eschatology of the Gospels*, London, 1912, p. 111f.

20. Outside the synoptic Gospels, distinction is rarely made between the Jewish people as a whole and its leaders (as, e.g., in Acts 3:17; but this is not the case with 1 Cor. 2:8). Ordinarily, the Jews are summarily referred to as murderers of Jesus and persecutors of the church (1 Thess. 2:14-18). Cf. F. Philippi, *Paulus und das Judentum*, Leipzig, 1916; W. Lütgert, "Die Juden im Neuen Testament," *Aus Schrift und Geschichte* (Festschrift Adolf Schlatter), Stuttgart, 1922.

21. In the Book of Acts, it is equally rare that the apostles heal without being asked. This is the case in the healing of Aeneas at Lydda (9:33-35), and of the father of Publius at Malta (28:8). The paralytic from Lystra already had faith (14:9; cf. note 23).

22. G. Baldensperger in the *Revue de Théologie et de Philosophie* (Lausanne), 1924, p. 190, states that the words in Mark 6:5, "and he could do no mighty work there, except that he laid his hands upon a few sick people and healed them," reveal the redactor's embarrassment. If this is correct, we must admit that the simple and original meaning of οὐκ ἐδύνατο was early misunderstood. Matthew (13:58), as is known, deletes the ἐδύνατο.

23. Πίστις in the synoptics: W. H. P. Hatch, "The Pauline Idea of Faith," *Harvard Theological Studies*, II, 1917, pp. 22-29; R. Gyllenberg, *Pistis* II, Helsingfors,

1922, pp. 76-83; M. Werner, *Der Einfluss paulinischer Theologie im Markusevangelium*, Giessen, 1923, pp. 122-126. The subject is divided into three groups: a) Utterances reflecting missionary terminology (to believe in the Gospel; in Jesus, the Messiah): Mark 1:15; 9:42; 13:21; 15:32; Luke 8:12; 18:8; 22:32; b) utterances concerning πίστις or ὀλιγοπιστία (in God) as Jesus intended it: Mark 4:40; Matt. 17:20 (which originally had no connection with miracle); 6:30; 8:26; 14:31; 16:8; c) faith and miracle: 1) the faith of those who were healed. Here πίστις is always confidence in the power of the thaumaturge. This is not the case in Acts. Peter declares, "And his name, by faith in his name, has made this man strong whom you see and know; and the faith which is through Jesus has given the man this perfect health in the presence of you all' (3:16). Here, faith is directed to the glorified Messiah, though we do not learn that the paralytic found faith. But in 14:9 it is expressly stated: "seeing that he had faith to be made well. . . ." In both cases, healing is a σημεῖον for unbelievers (cf. Acts 4:22: τὸ σημεῖον τοῦτο τῆς ἰάσεως); 2) the faith of the thaumaturge: Mark 9:14-29; 11:22ff.; cf. James 1:6. These reflections are obviously secondary.

24. At times, supernatural power is thought of as inherent in the thaumaturge, as somehow given with his very nature; at times it is thought to come from God or the demons. This last point of view prevails in the New Testament: God acts in and through Jesus; God, Christ and the Spirit operate through the apostles and other wonder-workers. The latter work their δύναμις by way of an imperative (ἀνάστηθι, ἔγειρε, καθαρίστητι), often invoking the name of Jesus (cf. Acts 3:16; 16:18; on the other hand, cf. 14:10). Curiously, Acts 9:34 offers us a word which is both a statement and an appeal: ἰᾶταί σε Ἰησοῦς Χριστός, directly followed by the imperative: ἀνάστηθι etc. In addition to the formula, which utters or omits the name of Jesus, there is the *prayer*, which does not *prepare* for but *provokes* the δύναμις. Apart from exorcism, in the church prayer gradually becomes the

normal means for producing miracle (regarding this development from formula to prayer, cf. S. Mowinckel, *Psalmenstudien* V, Oslo, 1924, pp. 30ff.). This actualizes the problem of *faith*. The earlier idea of supernatural power as inherent in the thaumaturge continues to thrive in the heart of early Christianity (Mark 5:30; Acts 5:15; 19:12).

25. It would be interesting to examine the ideas and notions of ancient Christian authors regarding magic, to explain how it related to Judaism and Hellenism, and then to study its specifically Christian nuance. There are a great many observations in L. Thorndike, *A History of Magic* I-II, London, 1923. Those who have tried to give an unequivocal definition of the connection between magic and religion are K. Beth, *Magie und Religion bei den Naturvölkern*, Tübingen, 1912; R. R. Marrett, "Magic," Hastings' *Encyclopedia of Religion and Ethics* VIII, 1915, pp. 245ff. (Here M. Gaster refers to Jewish magic); Gillis Wetter, *Religion och Magi*, Bibelforskaren (Uppsala), 1917; L. Deubner, *Magie und Religion*, Freiburg i. Br., 1922; S. Mowinckel gives a very exact and penetrating critique of these studies in his *Psalmenstudien*, pp. 59-75; V, pp. 14-18, Oslo, 1921, 1924.

26. Dibelius, *From Tradition to Gospel*, pp. 83ff., has clearly shown that the healing *technique* asserts itself especially in pure miracle narratives; he also explains the details of this technique. As to the means for healing, only spittle and oil are used (Mark 7:33; 8:23; 6:13). According to the popular notion, there is no contradiction between such means and the miraculous δύναμις, for these elements are vehicles of a divine healing power (cf. T. Canaan, "Aberglaube und Volksmedizin im Lande der Bibel," *Abhandl. des hamburg. Kolonialinstituts* XX, 12, Hamburg, 1914). On the other hand, Matthew appears intent on emphasizing that Jesus performed his healings by the *word* alone: the centurion declares (8:8), μόνον εἰπὲ λόγῳ, and directly thereafter the evangelist records that Jesus ἐξέβαλεν τὰ πνεύματα λόγῳ (8:16). Neither

Matthew nor Luke has preserved narratives which tell of using spittle.

27. On Simon Magus, cf. A. Wikenhauser, *Die Apostelgeschichte und ihr Geschichtswert*, pp. 394ff.; a list of literature to be consulted is appended.

28. Matt. 11:6 and Luke 7:23 are the object of a penetrating and valuable study by J. Lindblom: "Skandalon, Eine lexicalisch-exegetische Untersuchung," *Uppsala universitets årsskrift*, 2, (1921), p. 32f. Lindblom explains the words μακάριός ἐστιν ὃς ἐὰν μὴ σκανδαλισθῇ ἐν ἐμοί as follows: "Blessed is he for whom I am not such an occasion for falling that he does not believe in me." No doubt, this is a proper interpretation, but Lindblom encounters difficulties when he must give the *reason* for this unbelief. The difficulty is resolved if we assume a false interpretation has been given to Jesus' miracles. Doubt seizes even the Baptist when in his captivity he hears of Jesus' deeds.

29. Jewish exorcism is described by Josephus in Ant. VIII, 2, 5. On the use of Jesus' name by Jewish exorcists, cf. D. Chwolson, "Das letzte Passahmahl Christi," *Mémoires de l'acad. imp. des sciences de S. Pétersbourg* VII, 41, 1, Petersburg, 1892, pp. 100-107.

30. In *Zeitschrift für die neutestamentliche Wissenschaft* 1917/18, E. Boeklen expresses the opinion that the original story of the temptation allows for only two scenes, viz., the worship of Satan and the flight through the air. Infuriated because Jesus refuses to worship him, the devil tries to kill him by inducing him to hurl himself from the pinnacle of the temple in the confidence he has the miraculous help of God. But the sources disavow this construction and rob it of all foundation. It is evident that changing stones to bread and soaring through the air belong to the same miracle-category, which confirms the use of the same formula of introduction. To

our theory that the temptation story reflects the debate on miracle in the church it cannot be objected that Jesus later worked miracles he had previously refused to perform. For Jesus does not yet exercise his ministry as Savior and Revealer of God's power. In Matthew's version of the temptation story, he is merely the model for the disciple who is tempted. Naturally, we cannot prove with absolute certainty that the third temptation (on the mount) is a fragment of the original temptation story, a trace of which is still found in Mark. But we cannot deny this view a certain feasibility. First of all, Jesus experiences all the terrors of desert solitude in midst of the beasts; then he is carried to the high mountain, and after his experience, the marvelous view is calculated to be all the more tempting. On the change of scene from desert to mount, cf. my epilogue in Eitrem, *Die Versuchung Christi,* p. 30.

31. I do not believe with C. A. Bugge, *Das Problem der ältesten Kirchenverfassung,* Oslo, 1924, p. 19f., that Paul uses the term τέλειος in a purely technical sense, as denoting a higher degree of religious community. I side with R. Reitzenstein *(Die hellenistischen Mysterienreligionen,* 2nd ed., Berlin, 1920, p. 192) who paraphrases τέλειος with "voller Mensch." Cf. also K. Deissner, *Paulus und die Mystik seiner Zeit,* 2nd ed., Leipzig, 1921, pp. 39ff.

32. Cf. H. Windisch, *Taufe und Sünde im ältesten Christentum,* Tübingen, 1908, p. 123f.

33. It is true that the necessity for *practicing* charity is most often emphasized (James 2; 1 John 3:18, etc.). But it must also be said that a charitable action bereft of true charity is useless. Jesus taught this (Matt. 6:1-6), and it was a commonplace in Stoic diatribe; cf. G. Heinrici, *Die Bergpredigt begriffsgeschichtlich untersucht,* Leipzig, 1905, pp. 59ff.; *Theol. Stud. u. Krit.,* 1922, pp. 80ff.

34. On the use of the name and its power, cf. W. Heitmüller, *Im Namen Jesu*, Göttingen, 1903, p. 128f.

35. More often than not, commentators give a very vague
description of the persons represented by the tares
among the wheat. Thus A. Jülicher *(Gleichnisreden* II,
p. 555f.) describes them as "seducers and impious sorts,"
"false believers." But great sinners and those whose
transgressions were evident were excluded from the
sphere of the church (1 Cor. 5:2f.; Matt. 18:17f.). So
we must consider persons who could scarcely be distinguished from true believers. This thought draws our
attention precisely to the false prophets, to their prophecy, miracles, and exorcisms done in Jesus' name. Even
the terms of the parable's interpretation support our
thesis. The ζιζάνια are "the sons of the evil one" (Matt.
13:38)—those who commit ἀνομία—also called σκάνδαλα
(Matt. 13:41). The connection between ἀνομία and
σκάνδαλα is reminiscent of Psalm 140:9: φύλαξόν με ἀπὸ
παγίδος ἧς συνεστήσαντό μοι, καὶ ἀπὸ σκανδάλων τῶν ἐργαζομένων
τὴν ἀνομίαν (cf. S. Mowinckel, *Psalmenstudien* I, pp. 102,
122f., 173). For the use of σκάνδαλον in an apostrophe, cf.
Matt. 16:23.

36. For words compounded with ψευδο-, see Corssen,
Socrates, 1918, p. 106f.

37. No doubt, the idea of false prophet in primitive
Christianity would have developed as follows: a) the
thaumaturge who misuses Jesus' name out of cupidity;
b) the false prophet of the end-time, the servant of the
false Messiah; c) the heretic. Investigation of the origins of the second (eschatological) type and the conditions which explain it would merit a separate study (cf.
E. von Dobschütz, *Kommentar zu den Thessalonicher-
Briefen*, Göttingen, 1909, p. 295).

38. To tell the truth, antiquity could not psychologically
or concretely describe the true character of a false
prophet. Men saw in him either the covetousness of a

vulgar charlatan who seeks money and pleasure, or, satanic mischief, or both at the same time. O. Weinreich in his "Alexandros der Lügenprophet und seine Stellung in der Religiosität des II. Jahrhunderts nach Christus," *Neue Jahrbücher für das klassische Altertum* XXIV, 1921, p. 129f., undertakes an objective appraisal of this phenomenon. It even appears Paul was familiar with the notion of the pseudo-prophet, in spite of himself (cf. 1 Cor. 12:1-3). Or, we must rather interpret this passage as if the false prophet threw off his mask in the moment of ecstasy and cried out: ἀνάθεμα Ἰησοῦς. This second interpretation is more probable, considering the διάκρισις πνευμάτων (12:10), which tests not only the nature of the inspiration, but also the very personality of the prophet. Nonetheless, I should like to attempt another explanation of 1 Cor. 12:1-3, though with great reservation, limiting myself to showing its possibility. As soon as we ask, "Into what situation are the words ἀνάθεμα Ἰησοῦς naturally thrust?" the answer can only be that we have a *formula of renunciation* here by which a person separates himself from faith in Christ and protects himself from the suspicion of being a Christian (Luke 2:10: [εἰπεῖν] λόγον εἰς τὸν υἱὸν τοῦ ἀνθρώπου; Acts 26:11: ἠνάγκαζον βλασφημεῖν). 1 Cor. 12:1-3 obviously replies to a *special* question, before dealing in depth with the charismata theme. What was this special question? It is assumed that, under the pressure of synagogue discipline, a Jewish-Christian of Corinth could have been led to utter an ἀνάθεμα Ἰησοῦς. He later tried to excuse himself by giving out that he pronounced these fatal words under the influence of the Spirit (Mark 13:11). In order to refute this argument the apostle appeals to the Corinthians' experiences. When they were still heathen, they were prey to demonic powers, irresistibly won over to the εἴδωλα ἄφωνα, and can infer (διὸ) that whoever curses Jesus is swayed by the same demon. The apostle then does not stress the *passive state*, exclusive of man's resistance, for this point cannot support the assertion that "no one speaking by the Spirit of God ever says 'Jesus be cursed.' " On the contrary, stress is put on the "dumb idols." As the demonic spirit wins a man over to idols, so the Holy Spirit by an inner necessity leads us to Jesus and to God. The words, "no one speaking by the Spirit of God . . ." are thus a response to the church's question, has this brother been able to speak by the Spirit of God? Paul replies in a general formula, and as was his wont, reverses the proposition: No one can give this ecstatic witness and say κύριος Ἰησοῦς, except by the Holy Spirit. What is involved is a logical inversion of the first peremptory reply.

39. Apostolic Constitutions VIII, cf. O. Bardenhewer, *Geschichte der altkirchlichen Literatur* II, 2nd ed., Freiburg i. Br., 1914, p. 598f.; E. Hennecke in *Harnack-Ehrung*, Leipzig, 1921, p. 157f.

40. The idea that the miracles were important only for *unbelievers* has perhaps found some support in 1 Cor. 14:22: "Thus, tongues are a sign (σημεῖον) not for believers but for unbelievers. . . ."

41. Similar thoughts and formulas are found in Athanasius, Vita Antonii, chapter 38.

42. On miracles in the church, cf. R. Bückmann, *Zeitschrift für die gesamte lutherische Theologie und Kirche* XXXIX (1878), pp. 216-254; H. Werner and A. Jülicher in *Hermes* LIII (1918), p. 242f., and LIV (1919), p. 94f.